How to be Accountable Workbook

TAKE RESPONSIBILITY TO CHANGE YOUR BEHAVIOR, BOUNDARIES, AND RELATIONSHIPS

Faith G. Harper,
PhD, LPC-S, ACS, ACN

& Joe Biel

Microcosm Publishing
Portland, OR

HOW TO BE ACCOUNTABLE WORKBOOK

Take Responsibility to Change Your Behavior, Boundaries, and Relationships

Part of the 5 Minute Therapy Series

© Faith G. Harper, PhD, LPC-S, ACS, ACN &
Joe Biel

This edition © Microcosm Publishing, 2021

First edition, June 8th, 2021

ISBN 9781648410611

This is Microcosm #655

Cover and design by Joe Biel

Edited by Elly Blue

For a catalog, write or visit:
Microcosm Publishing
2752 N Williams Ave.
Portland, OR 97227
503-799-2698
www.Microcosm.Pub

These worksheets can be used on their own, or as a companion to **How to Be Accountable** by Dr. Faith G. Harper and Joe Biel.

These worksheets are free to reproduce but no more than two can be reproduced in a publication without expressed permission from the publisher.

To join the ranks of high-class stores that feature Microcosm titles, talk to your rep: In the U.S. **Como** (Atlantic), **Fujii** (Midwest), **Book Travelers West** (Pacific), **Turnaround** in Europe, **Manda/UTP** in Canada, **New South** in Australia, and **GPS** in Asia, India, Africa, and South America. Sold in the gift market by **Gifts of Nature** and **Faire**.

Did you know that you can buy our books directly from us at sliding scale rates? Support a small, independent publisher and pay less than Amazon's price at www.Microcosm.Pub

Global labor conditions are bad, and our roots in industrial Cleveland in the 70s and 80s made us appreciate the need to treat workers right. Therefore, our books are MADE IN THE USA.

MICROCOSM · PUBLISHING

Microcosm Publishing is Portland's most diversified publishing house and distributor with a focus on the colorful, authentic, and empowering. Our books and zines have put your power in your hands since 1996, equipping readers to make positive changes in their lives and in the world around them. Microcosm emphasizes skill-building, showing hidden histories, and fostering creativity through challenging conventional publishing wisdom with books and bookettes about DIY skills, food, bicycling, gender, self-care, and social justice. What was once a distro and record label was started by Joe Biel in his bedroom and has become among the oldest independent publishing houses in Portland, OR. We are a politically moderate, centrist publisher in a world that has inched to the right for the past 80 years.

TABLE OF CONTENTS

INTRODUCTION 7
S.T.O.P. Skill 16
T.I.P.P. Out of Crisis 17

UNDERSTAND YOUR BEHAVIOR 21
Accountability Self Assessment 24
Trauma Management Plan 30
Types of Triggers 34
Trigger Response Plan 36
Needs Inventory 40
Feelings Identification 42
Name your Emotions 45
Values Clarification 47
Map Your Values 51
My Authentic Self 52
Power Threat Meaning 53
Unpacking Then 55
Unpacking Now 59
Toxic Relational Patterns 61
The Inventory: How To Stop
Keeping Secrets From Yourself 70
Shadow Work 80
Shadow Work Questions for Introspection 81
Shadow Work Meditation 84
Shadow Work Self-Check-In 84

BARRIERS TO ACCOUNTABILITY 89
Thinking Errors 91
Cognitive Biases 97

CHANGE YOUR BEHAVIOR 103
Self-Compassion 104

When Presented With New Information 106
First Thought, Second Thought 107
Cognitive Defusion 111
Compassionate Accountability 114
How Can You Reframe Your Experience? 116
S.O.L.V.E. Your Problem 117
Figuring Out Our Stuck Points 119
Gratitude Journaling 120
Intention Setting 123
A Week of Intentionality 125
Accountability WOOP 127
Accountability Goal Setting 129
Progress Log 136
Achieve Your Goals 145
90-Day Skill Challenge 151

CHANGE YOUR RELATIONSHIPS 153
Relationships Inventory 154
Circle of Closeness 156
I Statements 157
The Four Levels of Communication 159
Apologies, Atonement, Forgiveness, and Repentance: Accountability in Action 161
The Three R's of An Apology 163
Gaslighting-Proof Yourself 165

PROBLEM SOLVING WITH OTHERS 167
Talking Out Conflict 173
Conflict in Groups 176
Therapy, Coaching, Mentoring, and Accountability Partnerships 179

CONCLUSION 187

COMMON BRAIN TRAPS

Cognitive distortions are ways that our mind convinces us of something that isn't true. These irrational thoughts are a common cause of maladaptive coping and toxic behaviors, used to reinforce negative thinking or emotions. We send ourselves bad data and convince ourselves that it's true. Then they keep us feeling bad about ourselves.

Always Being Right: You must constantly "prove" yourself to be correct even when it hurts others' feelings.

Blaming: You can't see your own problems, influence, or contributions. Everything is someone else's fault.

Disqualifying the Positive: You dismiss every inch of praise as undeserved, an attempt at flattery, or naïveté.

Emotional Reasoning: You believe that negative feelings expose the "true" nature of things and that reality is a reflection of emotionally linked thoughts.

Fallacy of Change: Everything will only get better when hypothetical cicumstances (outside of your control) change.

Fallacy of Fairness: You find others guilty when they don't follow your code of justice.

Jumping to Conclusions: You make negative assumptions with little or no evidence.

Filtering: You exclude information that does not conform to your already held beliefs and focus entirely on the negative.

Mind Reading: You "know" that others must be thinking the worst possible things about you.

Labeling and Mislabeling: You judge someone's entire character (or your own) based on a single mistake.

Magnification and Minimization: You make mountains out of molehills or vice versa.

Catastrophizing: You expect that unlikely, worst possible outcomes will come true.

Overgeneralization: You make broad judgments hastily without sufficient data.

Personalization: You take everything everyone doees or says personally, even if it has nothing to do with you.

Should Statements: You beat yourself up because you *always* could have done more. u

Dichotomous Reasoning: You believe that everything is "Always, Every, or Never." When someone that you admire makes a mistake, you now have contempt for them.

 © Joe Biel, 2019, JoeBiel.net, This poster and other infographics like it are available from www.Microcosm.Pub

INTRODUCTION

Accountability is the ownership of your choices and behaviors and the impact they have on the world, regardless of your intent. Accountability is aligning your patterns of behavior to your values. In this book, which is a companion to the bestselling *How to be Accountable: Take Responsibility to Change Your Behavior, Boundaries, & Relationships*, we are going to explore some additional exercises and skills that can help you to achieve these goals. You can read both or just one—whatever you prefer. The ideas overlap, but the content of each is different. The most important thing, and we cannot stress this enough, accountability is about yourself and only yourself. A group can hold standards of what is and is not acceptable behavior with each individual, but in most every case, attempts to hold other people accountable aren't a successful way to manipulate someone into doing very personal work. You do, however, get to decide what is and is not an acceptable way to treat yourself, which you manage through boundaries.

This book is for everyone, not just people who are running around doing crimes and assaults. We all have things in our life we want to change. Usually when someone uses the word "accountability," it's referring to holding someone else accountable but group efforts for this are painfully ineffective as a rule. So even when someone else wrongs or hurts you, we'd like you to focus on things that you can change in your own life—focusing on repeated patterns in your life or your habits that make you cringe. Because, again, the one person that you can change is yourself. And it's shocking how others notice and respond to this.

A friend told Joe a story the other day. After three days of dogged sexual pursuit, a man who had agreed to publish the friend's first book lured her into his hotel room to "get something," where he thrust his tongue into her mouth. He had power over her and seemingly was trying to use that to his advantage. She felt like he didn't even like her, just that he was on the prowl. She rejected his advances, but fifteen years later she still wonders what she should have done and carries those feelings of shaken confidence and deep doubt. The experience of someone else challenging her boundaries led her to believe the situation was somehow her fault. Even recalling these events, she questions if it was really an attack.

Her attacker was an esteemed figure in her community and good friends with people that she respected. So she sucked up her feelings and somehow she and her attacker continued to work together for several years while she blocked out the attack and attempted to be friends. It was a conditioned response taught to her in childhood that she felt obligated to smooth over conflict. When similar accusations surfaced about her next publisher, she went back to her attacker and asked him about republishing her second book. She had blocked out all of the bad shit he had done to her. Her attacker seemed worried that she would blackmail him, began apologizing, and asked her to agree not to tell anyone about the attack. At this point, she remembered everything and realized she wanted nothing to do with him. The unresolved trauma compounded and boiled over.

These events and her wondering how she should have responded play out in her brain fifteen years later. Her confidence took a big blow. She still wonders what the appropriate response is and why she didn't just punch him in the face. Instead, she felt frozen. Joe asked if the same thing happened today, would she punch him? She thinks she would, or at least might. She says that she would definitely look him straight in the eye and tell him that he cannot publish her book. After a few more minutes of reflection, she suspects that she'd shut down the situation before she even had the chance to punch anyone.

Ultimately, rumors surfaced about the same man behaving similarly within the same community and before long he and his publishing house disappeared. Yet, those events still haunt her and fundamentally changed how she makes decisions and comports herself. She made the decision to stop working with one-man publishing houses. She pays closer attention to how people behave and has less tolerance for bad behavior from people in her network. She couldn't control this other person but she could set community standards and live according to her own values, rather than those thrust upon her.

After Joe summarized this story back to her, she responded "It is oddly empowering. To read someone else writing it validates it, even though you're just repeating what I said." Writing out your own story can be healing in the same way.

While it would be nice to have a magic wand we could wave and change other people's behavior, we cannot. But you know what we can do? Change our own behavior, how we respond to others' behavior, and create boundaries that ultimately protect us. Of course, this doesn't protect us from our own pasts or make this person accountable to their own actions. Being attacked is never your fault, even if you find yourself frequently in this situation or you are extra vulnerable. Still, changing your attacker is a personal process within themselves. Joe asked the friend how the information should be available to warn others about this person. She didn't know. That's the more complicated situation. Ultimately the attacker fled the community, who is presumably safe from him, but where was he now? Is he still perpetrating the same behaviors? We don't know. This part of the resolution and restorative justice are ultimately where communities struggle the most.

When it comes down to it, people don't resist change. We resist being changed. Accountability cannot be bestowed upon us by someone else, no matter how well meaning they are or how much we love them. We have to be worn down enough by the toxic patterns in our lives to decide we want to do something about it.

Maybe your accountability is something individual. You've cheated on a partner or assaulted someone. Perhaps you want to stop feeling like a burden on your roommates. Or you want to stop smoking. Maybe you're always missing deadlines at work or don't like to have serious conversations about your relationship with your partner. Maybe every time someone argues with you on the Internet you threaten to kill their dog. Maybe you want to create a daily exercise routine or live a life of purpose and meaning. Maybe you're an angry drunk who does things you regret in the morning.

Or maybe it's more systemic than your direct interpersonal relationships. Perhaps you're coming to grips with something large and systemic like the racism, homophobia, transphobia, and prejudice that has been fed to so many of us in modern society and you want to address them so you can be a proactive ally to repair the harm you've caused.

No judgement of your issue or issues; you're not alone in having made decisions you regret. All that matters is that you want to change something and you're here.

So let's face why you're here. Most people aren't ready to be accountable until they've either hit rock bottom or alienated someone from their life that they deeply care about. Maybe your partner gave you an ultimatum. Or you realized that your drinking, anger, or unreliability is keeping you from the things that you care about. Or your community is coming after you with pitchforks. It's scary. It's real. You've successfully avoided responsibility up until now by promising to do better and/or making temporary changes. But now you have to put your money where your mouth is. One thing that's important to realize is that it may be too late to heal those particular relationships. **So do this work for yourself, not for other people or for specific relationships.**

Weirdly, the thing that very few books on the subject will tell you is that most human relationship behavior is just maladaptive stuff from your earlier life experiences. You didn't know how to get your needs met, so you figured out some clunky workarounds that, in adulthood, cause worse and worse damage each time you attempt them. Basically something went haywire at some point and you created coping behaviors that don't actually fulfill your relational needs in the long term. Needs like authentic, mutual, and healthy connections.

Everyone—including ourselves—has done things that they aren't proud of. Joe grew up as an undiagnosed autistic person, fumbling through the world in the dark with a light switch nowhere in sight. Joe wasn't given much in the way of moral guidance as a child and developed a lot of coping mechanisms that were not effective at fulfilling needs, nor particularly kind to other people.

These coping skills got us through at the time, but didn't serve to support healthy relationships as we get older. So we need to build new habits, instead of relying on old ways of being.

Joe was raised by a single mom with a dad confined to a wheelchair with his speech unrecognizably slurred. Their home was ruled by violence and confusion. Faith would refer to the result of this upbringing as an avoidant-fearful attachment style if we are going to use clinical language. Young Joe witnessed mom lying overtly about things both benign and important while also keeping secrets that deeply affected the family. Joe internalized the idea that you don't have to open up about even the most important things. As Joe grew up, it was easy to notice other kids forming friendships and developing emotional bonds while the same things were not happening for Joe. Coupled with maladaptive behavior, as an autistic person, the brain's mirror neurons are incapable of detecting when someone is attempting to subtly or nonverbally communicate a boundary. People would perceive Joe as inflexible and disrespectful of their boundaries even after they had expressed them. Joe was frequently alone as a result.

After the end of a number of long-term relationships, Joe finally came to understand that hiding intimate details created distrust. Joe also learned that people were communicating so much nonverbally. And they thought Joe was ignoring them. Joe spent years consciously working to learn the signs of other people's expressions and how to respond to them. Joe's first healthy, loving relationship was at 30 years old, where Joe could share openly and trust someone for the first time. Joe always knew that lying was wrong but withholding didn't seem like a form of dishonesty. Autistic brains can be confused by gray areas. But when Joe learned what was needed and made the decision to change, the quickly recognized toxic patterns were easy to eradicate. Dozens of apologies were issued to people that Joe had (however inadvertently) hurt in the past and Joe made a conscious decision to share everything, even things that look or sound foolish or might upset someone. Joe internalized the understanding that clear is kind. This is the process of becoming the person that you want (and need) to be.

Dr. Faith is a trauma therapist. In working with both victims and perpetrators, she has noticed similarities in their experiences. Many individuals who have offended recognize that they harmed themselves in the process of victimizing others. They have acted in ways that they have to live with for the rest of their lives, and in many cases have caused damage that can be healed but not repaired. It is the recognition of this harm that they need to work through.

Additionally, Faith recognizes that most perpetrators were victims of harm far before they caused harm to others. Not always, of course, but often. This means deep accountability work needs to take all of the complexities of our experiences of trauma into account, though most pundits may say otherwise. So this book endeavors to address all of these complexities in a way that you don't often see in the public sphere, or even in accountability literature.

As each of us began to write more and more about trauma, healing, and accountability, readers started reaching out requesting specific assistance on changing the behaviors they developed as a result of their traumatic histories. Joe received a lot of responses from autistic people seeking mentorship relationships. Five years later Joe finds coaching younger people to be a satisfying (albeit painful) way to revisit all of the mistakes learned the hard way.

We didn't intend to write a workbook (or a handbook!) but as we began looking for resources that could help people seeking this information, we found hundreds of books depicting the horrific acts of others and hundreds more detailing various ways that the author has been mistreated, but we found virtually nothing about how to end this cycle of abuse. People weren't asking us for first-person trauma porn narratives; they've already lived them. They were looking to change themselves.

There are some survivorship-based books that are structured for understanding relationship dynamics. While bell hooks' *All About Love* is the classic treatise on the subject and Lundy Bancroft's *Why Does He Do That?* offers a great support structure for survivors, there is remarkably little written about how to recognize and change patterns in our own behavior, which seems to suggest that change is only needed for people whose behavior is unfathomably worse than our own. But the reality is that everyone sees maladaptive behaviors in themselves that they'd like to change. While most discussions of accountability talk extensively about how to attempt to impose it on others, we can only control our own behavior, understand how it impacts others, make informed decisions about who to allow into our lives, and how to be accountable to ourselves.

Again, the only person you have control over is yourself. More and more people are recognizing this truth and reaching out for resources in a pretty resource-scarce market. So we took it on, which made us quickly realize that doing the topic justice is really difficult and there's probably a damn good reason no one else wanted to. Judging people and "cancelling" people is a way easier story to sell. Being flawed people grumpily doing difficult work, trying to support others doing the same, is really, really tough.

We too are flawed people who only got here through our own quests to do better. "Here" being the space of continuously working. Not done. Still flawed as fuck. The first steps are admitting it, recognizing it, making a decision to change the course of the behavior, and then creating a workable plan to make that happen. From there, you'll find that your shame withers, you have greater control over your life, you'll start to see yourself differently, and you'll establish a new way of interacting with the world.

The goal of this workbook is to give you the tools you need to understand why you behave the way you do, and to change whatever behaviors are no longer serving you. Hopefully along the way you'll also learn to truly appreciate yourself for who you are, improve your relationships, and achieve your goals.

You've got this!

But first….

This is hard work, so we're going to start with some skills that can help you deal with any difficult feelings and thoughts that come up as you work through this book.

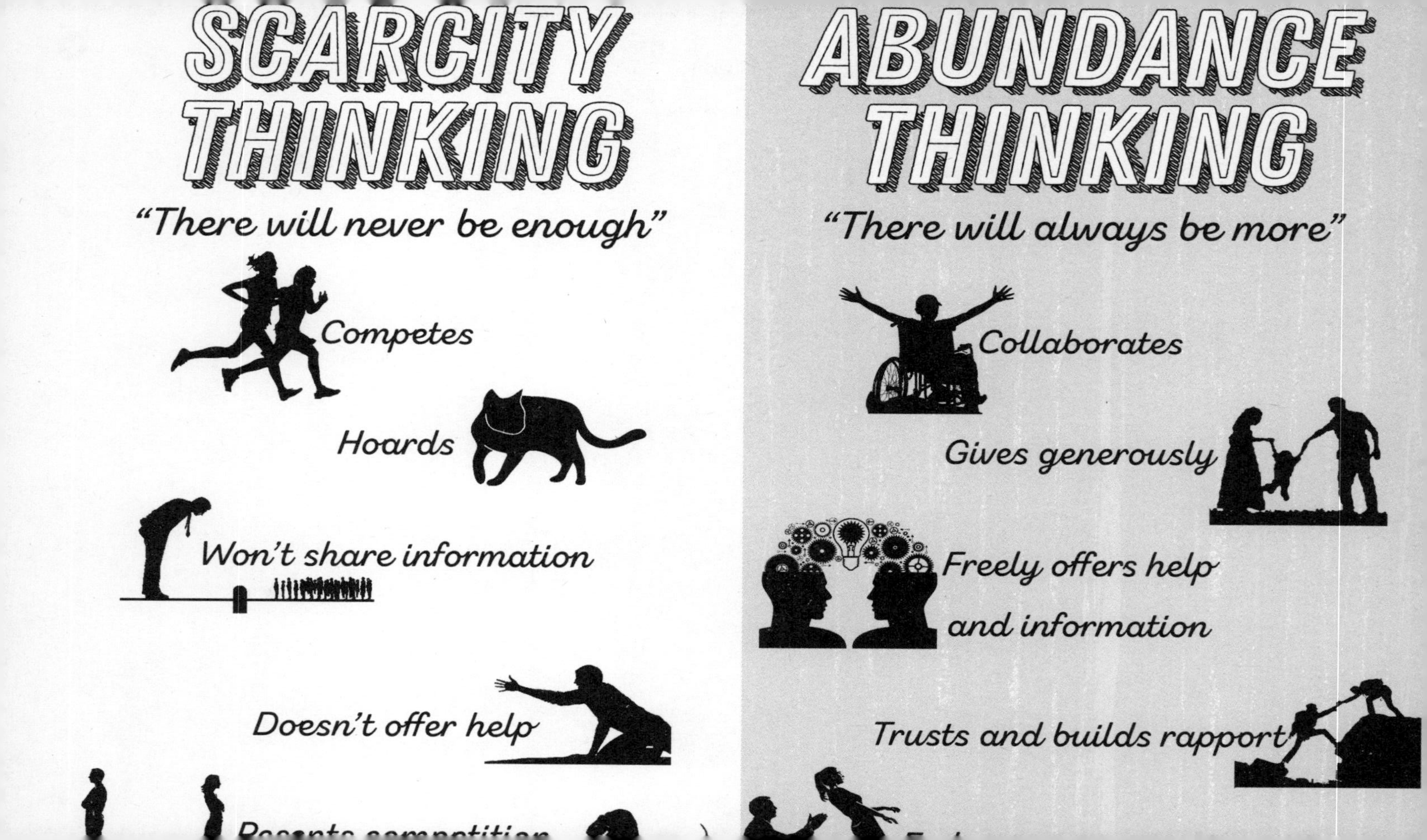

ABUNDANCE THINKING

"There will always be more"

- Collaborates
- Gives generously
- Freely offers help and information
- Trusts and builds rapport

SCARCITY THINKING

"There will never be enough"

- Competes
- Hoards
- Won't share information
- Doesn't offer help
- Resents competition

Strives to grow

Believes that the best is yet to come

Sees that the pie is growing

Thinks big

Embraces risk

Takes ownership of change

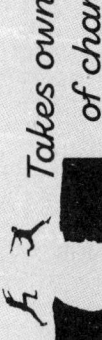

Fears being replaced

Believes times are tough

Believes that the pie is disappearing

Thinks small

Avoids risk

Fears change

Suspects others

© Joe Biel, 2019, JoeBiel.net, This poster and other infographics like it are available from www.Microcosm.Pub

STOP Skill

The STOP technique comes from Rob Stahl and Elisha Goldstein's work in Mindfulness Based Stress Reduction (MBSR). It is designed to help us manage stress in day to day interactions, but it is also hugely effective when used during times of intimacy when we find ourselves triggered or activated.

S — **Stop**. Rather than carrying on as if everything is fine when you are not, stop what you are doing for a moment to check back in with yourself.

T — **Take A Breath**. Seems intuitive, but it really isn't. When activated, we are far more likely to hold our breath or start breathing rapidly and shallowly. Take a deep breath, with an exhale that is longer than the inhale. This activates the body's parasympathetic system and has an immediate calming effect.

O — **Observe**. What's going on in your body? Any tension? Numbness? Just notice your somatic reactions instead of trying to disassociate from them.

P — **Proceed**. Now continue forward, regrounded in the present moment, at a level with which you are comfortable.

TIPP Out of Crisis

Another helpful exercise from DBT is an emotional regulation skill called TIPP, which stands for temperature, intense exercise, paced breathing, progressive muscle relaxation. This is a skill that is completely somatic...meaning body-based. When your mind has hit the overflow point, getting it calm again is most easily accomplished by starting with your body. Rebooting your nervous system then sends the signal to your brain of "ah, ok, I can chill out a little."

T — **Temperature**: We heat up when we get upset or are in a crisis, and changing your body temperature can signal to your system that it's okay to come down from its extreme state. Splash cold water on your face and wrists, stand in front of the air conditioner, squeeze an ice cube, or eat or drink something cool and see if that helps.

I — **Intense Exercise**: Release your excess energy, and give your body a sense that you're taking action in response to whatever is upsetting you. Run around the block, do jumping jacks, try a seven minute workout, run up the stairs, do a plank, whatever you can do.

P — **Paced Breathing**: Take slow, deep breaths to soothe your nervous system and take your nervous system out of fight/flight mode. You can count your breaths, count to five while you breathe in and seven while you breathe out, lie on the floor and do belly breathing, or any other breathing technique that works for you.

P — **Paired Muscle Relaxation**: This is another way to use your body to signal to your brain that you are safe, and to feel more grounded in your body. One by one, tighten and then relax each part of your body. Make fists with your hands, squeeze, then let them go. Move up your arms, tightening and relaxing, then up through your head, and down all the way to your toes.

How to Make a Decision

What is my desired outcome?

What is the simplest solution to achieve it? Is there an easier way?

Does my idea work for everybody involved? ◯ Y / N

Are the costs & consequences acceptable? ◯ Y / N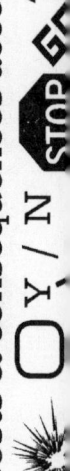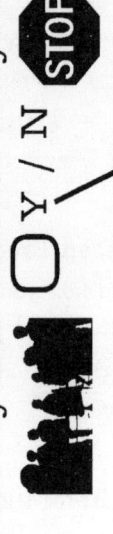

What are the worst, best, and likely outcomes? Can I manage them all?

☐ Y / N 🛑 GO↑

Does this decision cause harm to anyone I care about and/or our relationship?

☐ Y / N 🛑 GO↑

Does this decision take too much time and energy from the things I want and need to do?

☐ Y / N 🛑 GO↑

Could this decision cost more money than I can afford? Is there a cheaper way?

☐ Y / N 🛑 GO↑

DO IT!

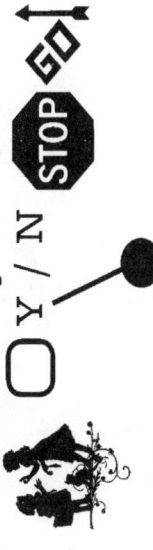

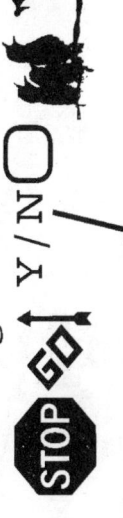

HOW TO RECOGNIZE WHAT YOU NEED

Hydrated?
When was your last drink of water?

Hungry?
When was your last meal? Last snack? Last protein?

Clean?
When was your last shower? Sometimes even it helps you feel better just to feel a bit more in control.

Dressed?
Putting on clean clothes that you didn't sleep in helps your mood. Give yourself permission to wear something that makes you feel like a million bucks.

When was the last time you complimented someone?
You will feel better when you are supportive and encouraging. It makes other people feel better and encourages them to repeat the gesture. Think of something really wonderful about someone that you haven't expressed before. Be genuine and thoughtful. No one around? Do it online.

Have you exercised?
Move your body to fun music. Be silly and dance around. Go for a run. Go to the gym if that's your thing.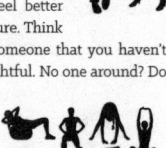

Last living contact?
For most people, sex is great and all but even a consensual cuddle or hug with someone that you care about—be it a lover, pet, friend, or family member—puts endorphins into your brain. And you'll make the other party feel better at the same time.

Need to talk about your problems?
Maybe you have a therapist. Maybe you have a friend, partner, or family member.

Tense?
When was the last time that you stretched? If you're not up for much, stand up and take a walk so your muscles don't atrophy.

Trouble sleeping?
Wear pajamas, get cozy in bed, and create a sleepy mood. Close your eyes for fifteen minutes. If you can't sleep, try writing about things on your mind or upsetting you.

Feel ineffective?
Take a break and focus on something that you can succeed at easily, however small. Focus on more and more difficult tasks till you feel in control of your destiny.

Feel unattractive?
Beauty is subjective. Everyone feels this way sometimes. Want proof? Post a picture of yourself to social media. Watch others compliment your appearance earnestly and endlessly.

Unable to make decisions?
Spend time making a plan for the day. If you still cannot act, put that problem aside for the moment and focus on something achievable until your confidence returns and you have new ideas.

Are you exhausted?
If you've overworked yourself emotionally, physically, mentally, socially, or intellectually, it takes days to recover sometimes. Give yourself a break. Rest and take in some entertainment.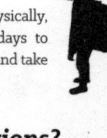

Have you changed medications?
Skipped doses? Forgotten a few protocols? These things will create great cognitive distortions and harm your mood. Give it a few days to shake out and try not to hold things against people.

Give it time.
Cognitive distortions ("everything is terrible and will never get better")  feel very real when they are happening but they are a terrible lens on reality. Worse, we cannot tell when we aren't thinking clearly. Don't buy into this lie, promise yourself not to stew on this perspective for a week, and look at how your perspective shifts.

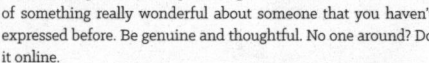

UNDERSTAND HOW YOU FEEL • SOLVE YOUR CRISIS

Stop comparing yourself to other people. Customize according to your own needs, abilities, and resources. Inspired by Sinope's 2015 list and licensed under a Creative Commons Attribution 4.0 International License. (eponis.tumblr.com/post/113798088670/everything-is-awful-and-im-not-okay-questions-to)
Joe Biel, 2019, JoeBiel.net, This poster and other infographics like it are available from www.Microcosm.Pub

Understand Your Behavior

Changing our behavior is far more difficult than just getting stern with ourselves in the mirror and saying "Self, stop your bullshit." All behaviors have a reason, even if they don't appear to right away. So the first part of this book is about uncovering where these adaptive strategies came from to begin with.

Before we begin, let's have a story.

In 2017, Pinegrove was the hottest indie band on the circuit. And then on November 21st of that year, singer/songwriter Evan Stephens Hall posted a long-winded, confusing, and vague confession about being sexually coercive with female fans. Then the band virtually disappeared for the next year. More questions emerged than answers. The line from the confession that stuck out the most was "I could sense who from the crowd would be interested in sleeping with me based on how they watched me perform." Just like the publisher who stuck his tongue down an author's throat, a musician has power over their fans. It's a situation where two people are not equals.

Over the next year, details began to emerge. A week before Hall posted his statement, Sheridan Allen, the founder of Punk Talks, an organization dedicated to offering therapy in the music scene, had demanded numerous parties—Pinegrove's label, management, the bands they were going on tour with, and a festival that they were performing at—by claiming to be a practicing therapist aware of "predatory and manipulative behavior toward women attending Pinegrove shows and women he has been sexually involved with." She asserted, "I hope you will stand with me on this, it has not been an easy time working directly to take down the biggest band in indie right now." She claimed to have knowledge of "multiple allegations" regarding Hall. Now this is odd because therapists don't normally threaten people, rather, they work with them on becoming their best selves, but we digress.

One by one, the dominoes fell, the bands fell off the tour, the label put the new album on hold, and the festival canceled Pinegrove. Hall posted the statement to the band's Facebook page and disappeared into therapy. A friend of the opening bands summarized disassociating from Pinegrove as "everyone has old shit that they don't want drudged up, so they flee situations like this before they are dragged through the mud as well."

When the dust settled and the details were revealed, there were two situations in question. The first was a consensual relationship with no misgivings where the other party repeatedly reiterated to Allen that Hall had no misdeeds. The other involved a fan expressing that Hall had practiced "verbal and contextual pressure" to get her to sleep with him despite her telling him she was in a committed relationship. Despite the stakeholders requesting these situations to be resolved privately, Allen pushed them into the light of public spectacle.

Now, stop right there. You've likely formed some opinions about these people and this situation. We've all been witness to these types of efforts to hold other people accountable. You have your opinions, so let's focus on the facts. Despite the incredibly unhelpful behavior of Sheridan Allen and Evan Hall's creepy admittance that he can tell which of his fans would be interested in sleeping with him, Hall took a break to understand his own behavior. He stopped. He reflected. He seemingly—dare we say—changed. It wasn't the death of his band, only a speed bump in his story...that ultimately resulted in him seemingly becoming a better person.

He took a cold, hard look in the mirror, and even though the accusations were exaggerated and did not align with his memory, he told Pitchfork "If she came away feeling bad about our encounter, feeling like she couldn't express how she was feeling honestly at the time, that's a huge problem." He explained that he felt defensive when he wrote the public statement and clarified that he categorically does not target fans for sex, but that this particular line was leveled against him by Allen so he had felt the need to acknowledge it. Hall told Pitchfork that he has been thinking about how consent applies to all relationships and how to live more democratically among peers. We don't know Hall, but his story is a common trope—people in the public sphere try to change for the best while people trying to help only cause further harm—but it's a new twist to move forward with positive change despite that and have people be able to accept this in the public sphere. This is relatively new in the field of accountability.

And fans see this. Rather than excommunicating Hall as a public figure for unconscionable behavior, people have welcomed the band back into their arms. A fan told the Washington Post, "I definitely feel that in a lot of situations, cancel culture doesn't help anyone, that it's a reductive and regressive way of addressing societal ills. Especially in Evan's situation, here's someone being very open, and honest, and vulnerable, and admitting that they probably did something wrong, and inviting criticism... So he's not Ryan Adams[1], right?" By February of 2019, the band resumed touring. While the confusion and the visage and spectre of Evan's past isn't erased, it is moving into the rear view.

When we are being individually challenged, even if it's in a less public way, the stakes feel impossibly high and it feels like we are the first person ever to have to deal with this. And while you always have to face yourself in some type of public arena, your struggles won't likely be reported in dozens of national media sources like Evan's are. So take twenty steps back, understand your behavior, and think about how it doesn't align with your values.

---

1   Ryan Adams, according to the New York Times, unapologetically got away with much manner of ugly behavior towards teenage fans for nearly two decades because, hey, artists just have aggressive tempers and entitlement to bad behavior..as long as they are a man.

Accountability Self Assessment

Let's start by seeing where you are right now. Not judgements, just looking to find ways to measure your progress while you do all this work (because it will show up again at the end of the book). You can build a more effective cupcake-reward plan that way.

Score each item on the Likert scale of 1-5: 1 never, 2 rarely, 3 sometimes, 4 most of the time, 5 always, and write some notes about why you chose that score.

I am aware of my personal value system, and work to act in accordance with these values.

1 —————— 2 —————— (3) —————— 4 —————— 5

> What is a personal value system?

I know what motivates me, and use those focal points to prioritize my time and energy.

1 —————— (2) —————— 3 —————— 4 —————— 5

> My usual sources don't always motivate me.

I follow through on expectations I set for myself, even if no one is watching me or checking in with me.

1 —————— (2) —————— 3 —————— 4 —————— 5

> I follow through on self-expectations more than I do for external expectations. Which still isn't often.

I honor my commitments to others, even if they are not watching me or checking in with me.

(1) —————— 2 —————— 3 —————— 4 —————— 5

> I just don't set reminders for myself, then I forget.

I set realistic timeframes to complete my commitments to myself and others. I have processes, timelines, and other methods to keep myself on task with the work I have prioritized.

1 —————— 2 —————— (3) —————— 4 —————— 5

> I set them, but don't follow through.

I accept full responsibility for the outcomes of my actions whether consequences are intentional or unintentional.

1 —————— 2 —————— 3 —————— (4) —————— 5

> Unfortunately, I repeat my mistakes.

I work with my own negative thoughts and feelings with compassion to prevent them from causing harm to myself and others.

1 —————— 2 —————— (3) —————— 4 —————— 5

> I've learned to have patience with myself, but sometimes lose my grip in the moment.

I have identified whose opinion I can trust and actively seek feedback from those people.

1 —————— (2) —————— 3 —————— 4 —————— 5

> I can't trust my mother, but I do trust my best friend. I think I need to find more people.

I accept constructive feedback even when it is uncomfortable and make appropriate adjustments to my behavior based on the feedback that has merit.

1 —————— (2) —————— 3 —————— 4 —————— 5

> I can accept constructive feedback if delivered in a calm manner, and I try to change what I can.

I evaluate my actions and the consequences of my actions regularly.

1 —————— 2 —————— 3 —————— (4) —————— 5

I focus on finding solutions rather than assigning blame.

1 —————— 2 —————— 3 —————— (4) —————— 5

I communicate with honesty.

1 —————— (2) —————— 3 —————— 4 —————— 5

I communicate with sincerity.

1 —————— 2 —————— 3 —————— (4) —————— 5

I endeavour to resolve conflicts directly with the concerned person or parties rather than complaining to third parties about the issue.

1 ——————— (2) ——————— 3 ——————— 4 ——————— 5

HOW TO THRIVE

 Read every day

 Respect/Compliment

 Embrace change

 Forgive

 Talk about ideas

HOW TO STARVE

 Compare self to others on Facebook every day

 Punch down/Criticize

 Fear change

 Hold a grudge

 Talk about people

Know it all

 Blame others for failures

 Feel entitled

 Never set goals

 Dictate others' experiences

 Internalize criticism

 Accept responsibility

Feel gratitude

 Have a long-term plan towards real goals

 Learn from people with different experiences

 Embrace meaning and purpose!

Trauma Management Plan

A trauma is anything that overwhelms our ability to cope. Some traumatic events hit us in such a way that we don't recover with time. And our brains encode that experience as an ongoing experience, and then tries to protect us by holding onto every possible sign that something might hurt us in the way we've been hurt in the past. And it doesn't take much for the switch to get flipped... places, people, smells, tones of voice, or even our thoughts.

As you've maybe already experienced, the topics in this book have the ability to bring up a lot of pain and old traumas. Especially if the reasons we've been behaving out of line with our values are themselves based in trauma. So let's look at how traume reactivates so we can create better strategies for working through these events.

So what's the mechanism of activating that old trauma script? It's a trigger, just like smelling hot buttered popcorn is a trigger for your salivary glands. A trigger is something that facilitates reliving a traumatic event. A trigger is something in the present that activates our memories of a past trauma in such a way that we are reliving that past moment in our present experience.

For example, a car brake squealing can make the brain freak out and make you think that you are getting hit by a car again. Or someone wearing the same scent as an abusive authority figure in your childhood can make all those feelings of anger or helplessness come back. That is your brain warning you that you might be in danger. It doesn't make you crazy, it makes you a survivor.

But it also means you are no longer in the present moment, dealing with present stimuli. It means your brain is playing the tape of whatever terrible shit happened to you in the past as a mechanism of trying to protect you in the present. Your brain just doesn't understand that the present is probably not as scary or dangerous as the recording.

Sometimes we limit ourselves by avoiding all possible triggers, which makes protective sense, but then we never heal. . And it's a crappy way to live and you deserve better. Instead, let's work on figuring out what's going on and developing new ways of being so we can live the lives we want for ourselves.

Use the next three exercises to evaluate your triggers and figure out what sets them off and the most effective ways to manage them.

Once you start putting a formal plan into place to manage your triggers, you will notice some stuff works great, some stuff not at all, and new ideas may come up that you want to incorporate. You may also get feedback from the people you love and trust. Make any notes that you want to remember here, too.

When you are feeling the most healthy, happy, joyful, and well what does life look like? *How do you spend your days? How do you feel? How do you interact with others? What do you like to do?*

> I'm in school, pursuing interests with the help of my best friend. We go on adventures together, and I get dressed up in fun costumes.

What things have you noticed help you manage your triggers more effectively in a general sense? *How much sleep do you need? How much exercise is beneficial? What should you be eating? Do you need to pray, meditate, or see certain people more/less often? What activities help?*

> Music with headphones, time with friends, designing my ideal life

What things from this list can you commit to doing regularly to help maintain equilibrium? *List 1-5 things you aren't doing regularly right now that you know would really help.*

> Showering frequently, spending time outside, playing piano

What are some of the situations that you have come to realize are triggers for you? *Rather than big, catastrophic things, think of things that happen on a more regular basis. E.g. "being in a crowded room" or "not doing well on a project," holidays or birthdays, smells, sounds, or voices. We don't know all of our triggers and may get triggered without any idea of what caused it but if you keep notes, you can often figure them out. Consider this list a work in progress.*

> Yelling, being trapped, jokes about my hospitalization or mental crises, being gaslit (even teasingly), condescendsion.

What are your early warning signs that you may be getting triggered? *What kinds of thoughts do you have? What emotions arise? What kind of behaviors do you engage in that you don't typically do?*

> Tripping over words, doubting myself, feeling antagonized

If you are triggered, what are the things you can do for yourself to help you manage your response to these triggers? *These are things you already do that become especially important in these situations but may also be coping skills or activities that you use when you are in especially tough situations. Faith wrote a whole book on the subject, Coping Skills.*

What do you need from others in terms of support? *You need help from others, especially if you are working on your intimate relationships. Who do you trust to provide that support? How will you ask them about it?*

How will you know that you have been triggered past the point that you, and the individuals who traditionally support you, can handle? *What will you notice in terms of your behaviors? Your feelings? Your thoughts? What should you and the people who support you watch out for?*

If you are at a point at which you are not able to manage these triggers on your own, or with the assistance of the people who traditionally support you, what is the next step for you? *Do you have treatment professionals that should be contacted? Crisis lines you prefer? A hospital you prefer, if needed? What resources are available to provide additional support?*

Once your crisis has been managed, how will you know when you are feeling **safe and secure again?** *What does restabilization look like for you? How can you communicate that to the people who may be worried about you?*

Types of Triggers

Now that we have a plan for how to manage being triggered, it can be helpful to go a bit deeper and figure out what our different types of triggers are.

True Triggers: That pre-thought wordless terror. It's a body based, felt-sense reaction that we often don't even recognize until after the fact. The best way to handle a true trigger is to simply notice its existence and use skills to ground ourselves and bring our bodies back to safety.

Distressing Reminders: These are things that call up memories of the trauma and cause awful feelings but through which we can still think and function. A lot of times we can describe what we are feeling even if we can't explain it. The best way to handle a distressing reminder is to soothe yourself when you are experiencing it.

Uncomfortable Associations: These occur when something that would otherwise be pleasant or at least neutral has an association to our trauma. We are able to manage these associations by consciously reframing them.

Trigger Response Plan

Now that you have an idea about the different types of triggers you are experiencing, you can create a plan to manage them. Practicing coping while you are not being triggered will help you remember what works when you need to. Try using coping and grounding skills from the introduction exercises that are specific to your types of triggers and rate how they worked so you can start to develop a more specific plan of attack for dealing with them.

True Triggers

Trigger	Coping Skill	Effectiveness

Distressing Reminders

Trigger	Coping Skill	Effectiveness

Uncomfortable Associations

Trigger	Coping Skill	Effectiveness

HOW TO RECOGNIZE WHAT YOU NEED

Hydrated?
When was your last drink of water?

Hungry?
When was your last meal? Last snack? Last protein?

Clean?
When was your last shower? Sometimes even it helps you feel better just to feel a bit more in control.

Dressed?
Putting on clean clothes that you didn't sleep in helps your mood. Give yourself permission to wear something that makes you feel like a million bucks.

When was the last time you complimented someone?

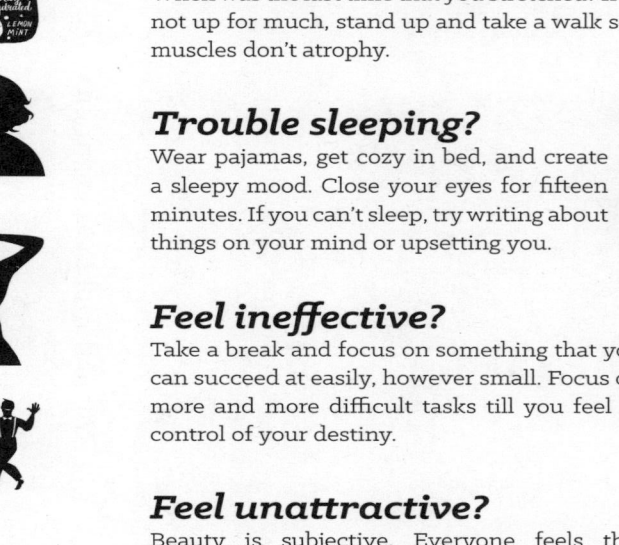

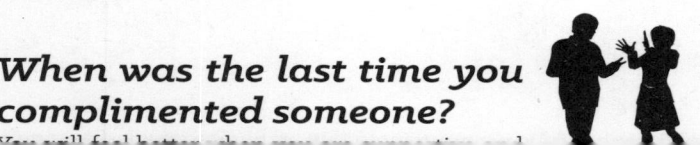

Tense?
When was the last time that you stretched? If you're not up for much, stand up and take a walk so your muscles don't atrophy.

Trouble sleeping?
Wear pajamas, get cozy in bed, and create a sleepy mood. Close your eyes for fifteen minutes. If you can't sleep, try writing about things on your mind or upsetting you.

Feel ineffective?
Take a break and focus on something that you can succeed at easily, however small. Focus on more and more difficult tasks till you feel in control of your destiny.

Feel unattractive?
Beauty is subjective. Everyone feels this way sometimes. Want proof? Post a picture of yourself to social media. Watch others compliment your appearance earnestly and endlessly.

until your confidence returns and you have new ideas.

Are you exhausted?

If you've overworked yourself emotionally, physically, mentally, socially, or intellectually, it takes days to recover sometimes. Give yourself a break. Rest and take in some entertainment.

Have you changed medications?

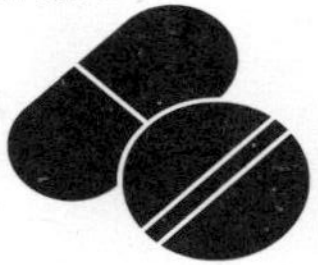

Skipped doses? Forgotten a few protocols? These things will create great cognitive distortions and harm your mood. Give it a few days to shake out and try not to hold things against people.

Give it time.

Cognitive distortions ("everything is terrible and will never get better") feel very real when they are happening but they are a terrible lens on reality. Worse, we cannot tell when we aren't thinking clearly. Don't buy into this lie, promise yourself not to stew on this perspective for a week, and look at how your perspective shifts.

expressed before. Be genuine and thoughtful. No one else around? Do it online.

Have you exercised?

Move your body to fun music. Be silly and dance around. Go for a run. Go to the gym if that's your thing.

Last living contact?

For most people, sex is great and all but even a consensual cuddle or hug with someone that you care about—be it a lover, pet, friend, or family member—puts endorphins into your brain. And you'll make the other party feel better at the same time.

Need to talk about your problems?

Maybe you have a therapist. Maybe you have a friend, partner, or family member.

UNDERSTAND HOW YOU FEEL • SOLVE YOUR CRISIS

Stop comparing yourself to other people. Customize according to your own needs, abilities, and resources. Inspired by Sinope's 2015 list and licensed under a Creative Commons Attribution 4.0 International License. (eponis.tumblr.com/post/113798088670/everything-is-awful-and-im-not-okay-questions-to) Joe Biel, 2019, JoeBiel.net, This poster and other infographics like it are available from www.Microcosm.Pub

Needs Inventory

We all have needs. Needs are different from wants in that they are essential to our survival, not just our comfort or desire. You may want a burrito (because delicious). But what you need is food to provide energy to the cells of your body, and a burrito could do that, but so could kale, despite your feelings about it. Sometimes what we want can confuse us about what we need, and sometimes our weirdest wants are a signal that we may have an unmet need that we don't know how to fulfill in a healthy way. Like the person who grew up in a family where they weren't allowed to express themselves who now picks fights over everything they consider "disrespect."

Understanding your needs is a good place to start. Having a need doesn't obligate any specific person to provide it to you, but knowing what matters to you gives you the tools to ask for your needs to be met, and to filter out people who disregard or disrespect those needs.

The following list of potential needs isn't complete or universal, but it's a good place to start in considering what is most essential for you.

CONNECTION
acceptance
affection
appreciation
belonging
cooperation
communication
closeness
community
companionship
compassion
consideration
consistency
empathy
inclusion
intimacy
love
mutuality
nurturing
respect/self-respect
safety
security
stability
support
to know and be known
to see and be seen
to understand and be understood
trust
warmth

HONESTY
authenticity
integrity
presence

PLAY
joy
humor

PHYSICAL WELL-BEING
air
food
movement/exercise
rest/sleep
sexual expression
safety
shelter
touch
water

PEACE
beauty
communion
ease
equality
harmony
inspiration
order

MEANING
awareness
celebration of life
challenge
clarity
competence
consciousness
contribution
creativity
discovery
efficacy
effectiveness
growth
hope
learning
mourning
participation
purpose
self-expression
stimulation
to matter
understanding

AUTONOMY
choice
freedom
independence
space
spontaneity

(c) 2005 by Center for Nonviolent Communication
Website: www.cnvc.org Email: cnvc@cnvc.org
Phone: +1.505-244-4041

Read through those lists of possible needs. For each column, make a list of things that are non-negotiable, things that make you happy and are nice, and things that are important to other people but you don't care about. You can use the list on this page for inspiration, and add your own.

Things I need	Things I want	Things that aren't important to me

Feelings Identification

Our emotions (also known as our feelings) are very similar to our thoughts but can be harder to pin down. And if we deal with anxiety on a constant basis, it's so overwhelming that anything else going on underneath tends to go unnoticed. But these other feelings could be what's activating the anxiety. Or they could be symptoms of other issues that also need your attention and care. Since a thought is just something that your brain tells you, you already know the words to use. But emotions are a different form of communication from inside our bodies and brains, so we have to learn the language to describe them.

Here is a list to get you started, but you can also search online for a "feelings wheel" or add your own to this list.

FEELINGS WHEN YOUR NEEDS ARE SATISFIED

AFFECTIONATE
compassionate
friendly
loving
open hearted
sympathetic
tender
warm

ENGAGED
absorbed
alert
curious
engrossed
enchanted
entranced
fascinated
interested
intrigued
involved
spellbound
stimulated

CONFIDENT
empowered
open
proud
safe
secure

EXCITED
amazed
animated
ardent
aroused
astonished
dazzled
eager
energetic
enthusiastic
giddy
invigorated
lively
passionate
surprised
vibrant

HOPEFUL
expectant
encouraged
optimistic

GRATEFUL
appreciative
moved
thankful
touched

INSPIRED
amazed
awed
wonder

JOYFUL
amused
delighted
glad
happy
jubilant
pleased
tickled

EXHILARATED
blissful
ecstatic
elated
enthralled
exuberant
radiant
rapturous
thrilled

REFRESHED
enlivened
rejuvenated
renewed
rested
restored
revived

PEACEFUL
calm
clear headed
comfortable
centered
content
equanimous
fulfilled
mellow
quiet
relaxed
relieved
satisfied
serene
still
tranquil
trusting

FEELINGS WHEN YOUR NEEDS ARE NOT SATISFIED

ANGRY
enraged
furious
incensed
indignant
irate
livid
outraged
resentful

ANNOYED
aggravated
dismayed
disgruntled
displeased
exasperated
frustrated
impatient
irritated
irked

AVERSION
animosity
appalled
contempt
disgusted
dislike
hate
horrified
hostile
repulsed

DISCONNECTED
alienated
aloof
apathetic
bored
cold
detached
distant
distracted
indifferent
numb
removed
uninterested
withdrawn

AFRAID
apprehensive
dread
foreboding
frightened
mistrustful
panicked
petrified
scared
suspicious
terrified
wary
worried

CONFUSED
ambivalent
baffled
bewildered
dazed
hesitant
lost
mystified
perplexed
puzzled
torn

DISQUIET
agitated
alarmed
discombobulated
disconcerted
disturbed
perturbed
rattled
restless
shocked
startled
surprised
troubled
turbulent
turmoil
uncomfortable
uneasy
unnerved
unsettled
upset

SAD
depressed
dejected
despair
despondent
disappointed
discouraged
disheartened
forlorn
gloomy
heavy hearted
hopeless
melancholy
unhappy
wretched

EMBARRASSED
ashamed
chagrined
flustered
guilty
mortified
self-conscious

FATIGUE
beat
burnt out
depleted
exhausted
lethargic
listless
sleepy
tired
weary
worn out

PAIN
agony
anguished
bereaved
devastated
grief
heartbroken
hurt
lonely
miserable
regretful
remorseful

TENSE
anxious
cranky
distressed
distraught
edgy
fidgety
frazzled
irritable
jittery
nervous
overwhelmed
restless
stressed out

VULNERABLE
fragile
guarded
helpless
insecure
leery
reserved
sensitive
shaky

YEARNING
envious
jealous
longing
nostalgic
pining
wistful
incensed
indignant

(c) 2005 by Center for Nonviolent Communication
Website: www.cnvc.org Email: cnvc@cnvc.org
Phone: +1.505-244-4041

Name your Emotions

In this exercise we will tease out the physical, visual, and mental manifestations of your primary emotions. Next to each dot, list an emotion that you frequently experience. Then list everything that you associate with that emotion. Feel free to start with anxiety, that's the big one you are working on right now...

But don't forget the other ones! E.g. "When I'm angry, I think that everyone has betrayed me and I want to smash things. People notice that my face tenses and keep their distance."

By each dot below, list an emotion and then make some notes about how you know that you are experiencing these emotions.

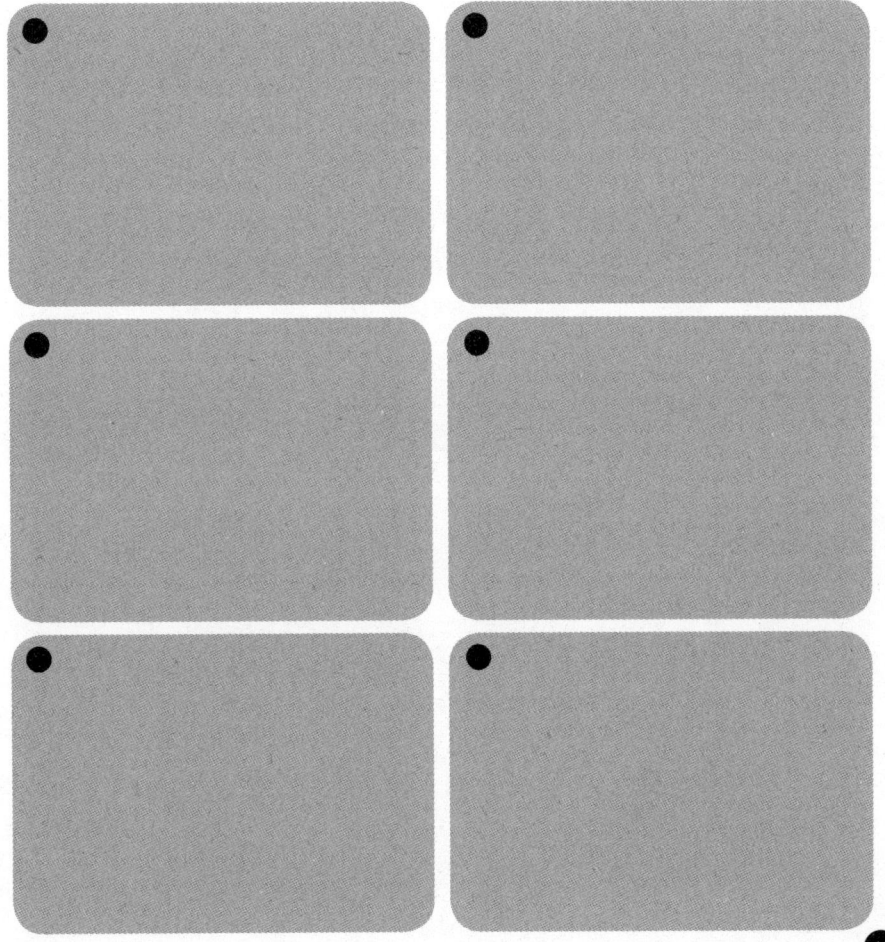

You will often feel a disconnect or a betrayal between your body and your mind as values from your upbringing are instilling feelings that you don't want to have because they aren't consistent with how you see the world now. If you were taught that you should always respect authority figures but one routinely insults you, your feelings will tell you when your actions are not in line with your values. Sit with your feelings and process what is going on in your body and mind. This is how you work them out of your life. What are some examples of this in your life now?

Make a list of events or behaviors that frequently cause those emotions, rating each one 1-10 on the scale of unpleasantness, using the SUDs scale from the first exercise.

What do you appreciate or need when experiencing each feeling? What is the useful information?

Values Clarification

In the accompanying handbook, we tell the story of the most engaging and controversial ever on social media—arguing about the color of Cecilia Bleasdale's dress. Was it white with gold lace or blue with black lace? Our perceptions are determined by our prior experiences. The dress is a good example because it's something we have no material investment in—yet millions of people took to arguing about it.

Just like how we have no control over how we interpret the colors of the dress, our prior experiences affect our values, beliefs, and attitudes in the same way. Nobody chooses how we interpret the world, which is why we need to stop, pause, reflect, and make conscious choices about how we carry out our values.

Many people don't have a language to articulate their values. So here's a huge list of potential values (plus space to write in more of your own).

Acceptance	Boldness	Compassion for animals
Badassitude	Bravery	Compassion for fellow humans
Accountability	Brilliance	
Accuracy	Calm	Competence
Achievement	Candor	Concentration
Adaptability	Carefulness	Confidence
Advocacy	Certainty	Connection
Allyship	Challenge	Consciousness
Ambition	Clean	Consistency
Artistic expression	Clear	Contentment
Artistic interactions	Clever	Contribution
Assertive	Comfort	Control
Attentive	Commitment	Convenience
Balance	Common sense	Conviction
Beauty	Communication	Cool
	Community	Cooperation

Courage	Social Justice	Greatness
Courtesy	Ethical	Growth
Creation	Excellence	Happiness
Creativity	Experience	Hard work
Credibility	Exploration	Tenacity
Curiosity	Expressive	Hard-working
Decisiveness	Fairness	Harmony
Defeating fascism	Family	Health
Dependability	Fame	Honesty
Design	Fearless	Honor
Determination	Feelings	Hope
Development	Feminism	Humility
Devotion	Intersectionality	Humor
Dignity	Ferocious	Hygge
Discipline	Fidelity	Imagination
Discovery	Focus	Independence
Dismantling oppressive systems	Foresight	Individuality
	Fortitude	Influence
Dynamic	Freedom	Innovation
Effective	Friendship	Insight
Efficient	Fun	Inspiring
Empathy	Generosity	Integrity
Empowerment	Genius	Intelligence
Endurance	Giving	Intensity
Energy	Goodness	Intuition
Enjoyment	Grace	Irreverent
Enthusiasm	Gratitude	Joy

Justice	Physicality	Self-care
Kindness	Playfulness	Self-compassion
Knowledge	Poise	Self-reliance
Lawful	Potential	Selflessness
Leadership	Power	Sensitivity
Learning	Practical	Serenity
Logic	Present	Service
Love	Productivity	Sexuality
Loyalty	Professionalism	Sharing
Magic	Prosperity	Silence
Mastery	Purpose	Simplicity
Maturity	Queerness	Sincerity
Meaning	Questioning authority	Skill
Moderation	Realistic	Solitude
Motivation	Reason	Spiritual
Nazi-Punching	Recognition	Spontaneous
Nesting	Reflective	Stability
Neutrality	Relaxation	Status
Openness	Representation	Stewardship
Optimism	Respect	Storytelling
Organization	Responsibility	Strength
Originality	Results-oriented	Structure
Passion	Righteousness	Success
Patience	Rigor	Support
Peace	Risk	Surprise
Performance	Satisfaction	Tree-hugging
Persistence	Security	Teamwork

- Sobriety
- Thorough
- Thoughtful
- Timeliness
- Tolerance
- Toughness
- Traditional
- Transparency
- Trust
- Truth
- Understanding
- Uniqueness
- Unity
- Vigor
- Vision
- Vulnerability
- Wealth
- Welcoming
- Winning
- Wisdom
- Wonder

Have values that aren't on this list? Write in your own.

Map Your Values

Values from the People who Raised Me (Parents, Guardians, Other Family Members, etc.)

Values from Other Important People in My Life (Friends, Partners)

Values Specific to my Local Community/Cultural Heritage

Values From my Larger Community

Values I Would Most Like to Live by

Values I Am Currently Living by

My Authentic Self

Here's a place to take the core elements of the work you did regarding your personal values to create a snapshot of your essential identity.

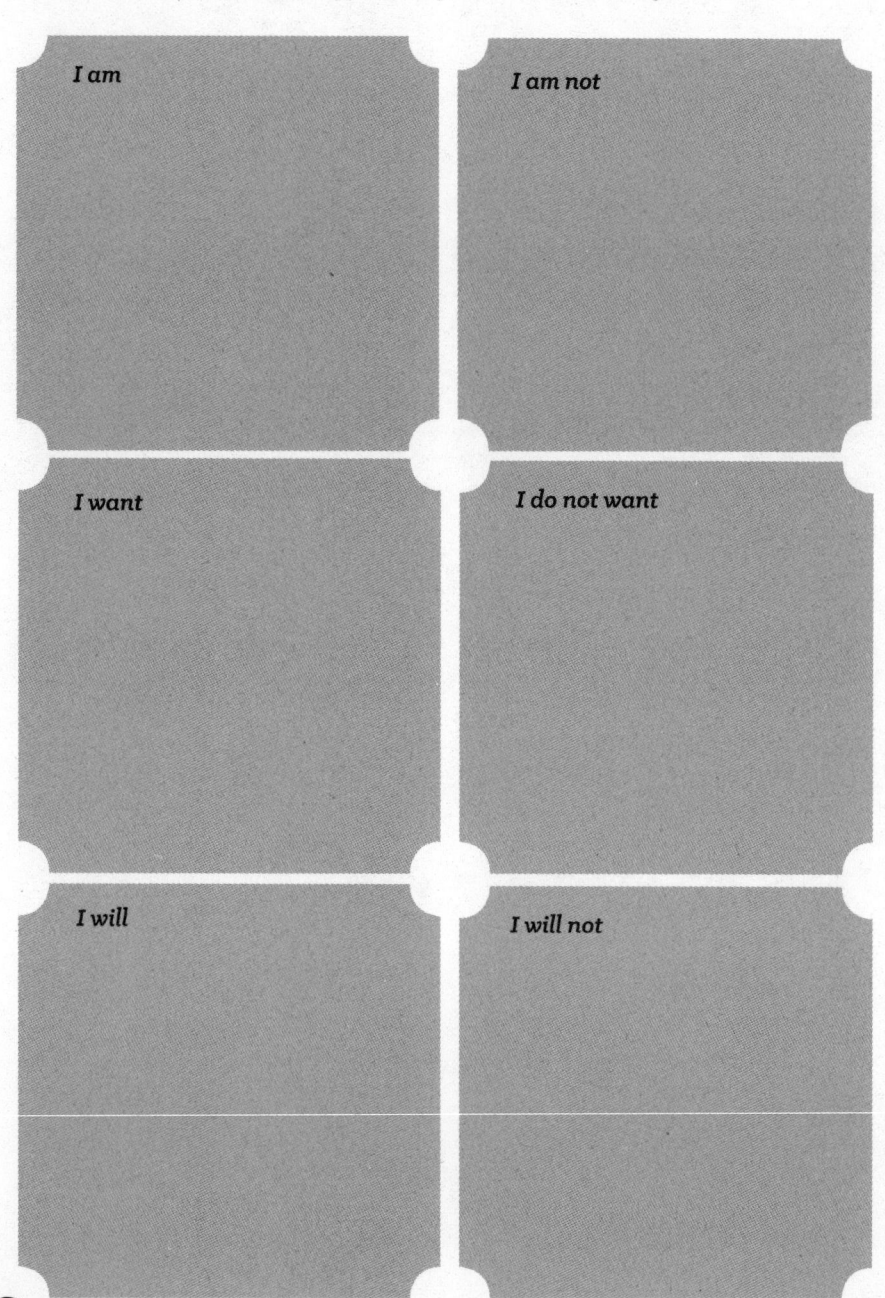

I am

I am not

I want

I do not want

I will

I will not

Power Threat Meaning

Taking accountability for your actions doesn't mean "I'm just a piece of shit." And recognizing the influences in your life on your interactions doesn't excuse your shitty behavior either. There's an old Polish proverb which translates to "Not my circus, not my monkey." When it comes to how our past experiences have shaped us into being prickly, sneaky, defensive and otherwise crappy-acting, however it's a little bit more complicated. Faith tells her clients "Maybe you didn't buy the ticket, but it is now your circus and your monkeys." So this section isn't about excusing anything...but figuring out how you ended up with that ticket in hand.

So you know how most therapy and trauma healing and stuff is about figuring out what is not working in your brain and teaching you coping skills and new tricks to make it work? And how they tell you that even if you feel like the rest of the world is crazy, the real answer to your own behavior, feelings, and thinking lies within your own mental processes, self-control, and agency?

What if that weren't true? What if your brain is doing exactly what a healthy brain is designed to do. . . just in response to a threat? What if the trauma you have experienced, coupled with the power dynamics in the world around you are the problem, not you? Maybe we didn't buy the ticket but it is now, officially, both our circus and our monkey.

Here's a framework that was developed by a bunch of smart people for figuring out why your brain is freaking out at you:

It's called the Power Threat Meaning (PTM) framework and it says that threatening power dynamics experienced during your brain's development or adulthood have created systems in your brain that produce the symptoms leading to your diagnosis. For example, if you have social anxiety, it's probably due to your early experiences, maybe coupled with some predisposition to an anxiety disorder. If we considered the whole context of your life, we'd probably treat you a lot differently than just based on a diagnosis.

So how does the PTM framework work? It starts by asking the following questions:

How has power operated in your life? What kinds of things happened to you because power was wielded over you in harmful ways? This could be anything from growing up with a domineering parent to experiencing systemic racism to living through a war.

What kinds of threats did this pose to you? How did this harmful use of power against you cause harm to you or otherwise affect you? For instance, maybe now you can't stand being around someone yelling, or maybe you lost a leg.

What meaning did you develop based on these situations and experiences to you? How did you make sense of these experiences? What did they tell you about the world and other people in it? Maybe you learned that all people in authority are potential threats to your safety, or that loud bangs mean you or someone around you will be hurt or killed.

What kind of threat response did you develop due to these events? What did you do to survive? How did you cope? How did you behave to protect yourself? So now you literally don't hear someone's words when they're yelling, or you feel compelled to physically attack any sort of authority figure.

Unpacking Then

What events in your life had a negative impact on you? In other words, what scared you, threatened your security, harmed you or traumatized you? It's generally easier to compile this as a timeline in five-year increments because it can be hard to remember things in great detail, especially from periods where we were really young and/or there was a lot going on. Keep in mind that sometimes terrible things are normalized around us to the point that we don't even register them as traumatic.

What events had an impact on your parents and other caregivers?

How did those events inform their interactions with you?

What social systems were in place that exacerbated these negative experiences?

What social systems are in place that continue to operate as a barrier to healing in the present?

What were the consequences of your negative life events?

How did these events impact your daily life? Surroundings?

How did they impact your relationships at that time?

How did they impact your physical body?

How did they impact your view of yourself? What feelings did you notice? What did you tell yourself about your experience?

How did they impact your behaviors? Meaning...what did you need to do to survive?

What rules did you figure out about how the world works based on these events?

How did you come to define "normal" based on these experiences?

What labels were used to describe you (diagnoses, things people called you based on your behavior)?

Which of these labels are still used to describe you, either by others or by your internal voice?

How did you expect others to treat you and/or interact with you? We don't exist in isolation, but in interactions with others which we then use to create rules about the world. These rules are often in the form of "If I _____, other people will _____." Write down the rules you've learned:

If I am hurt, other people will: _____

_____

If I am scared, other people will: _____

_____

If I am angry, other people will: _____

_____

If I am peaceful, other people will: _____

_____

If I am honest, other people will: _____

_____

If I am expressive, other people will: _____

_____

If I am… _____

_____

Unpacking Now

How does this all fit together to inform your present reality? What is your story of survival?

What skills did you develop to survive? Both in your external works and your internal understanding of these events?

What labels or descriptions best describe your experience?

What social and political systems are in place that limit your access to healing and wellness?

What makes you strong?

How do you demonstrate your strength?

What abilities do you have that you didn't have in the past?

What resources do you have that you didn't have in the past?

What power do you have that cannot be taken from you regardless of your circumstances?

How would you describe who and where you are at this moment in your life?

What areas do you want to build strength in?

What would your life look like if things were ideal for you?

What systems changes would support that process?

What work do you need to do for your own self growth?

What assistance do you need from others that is in their power to provide?

What resources do you need to access?

Toxic Relational Patterns

What are cognitive distortions? A thought we had that we decided to hold on to as a truth...even when it's not that true, and not that helpful. It's a story we've become attached to and act from. And it ends up causing problems. Typically when we read about cognitive distortions and common thinking errors, we are focused on the types of thought patterns that lead to a spiraling of depression and anxiety. But there are other kinds of thinking errors (and their accompanying behavioral patterns) that have just as large an impact on ourselves and an even larger impact on our relationships with others. The term toxic relational strategies means not just how we think in certain circumstances, but how we interact with others based on those thinking patterns.

These are behaviors everyone is capable of. Everyone has engaged in some of these strategies at some point in their lives. And we have all been victims of these strategies. Not just from perpetrators of abuse, but from otherwise good people who engaged with us in unhealthy ways because they thought that was the best way to meet their needs. The difference is in the degree in which we undertake them.

The purpose of this exercise is to look at patterns of interactions in our own lives, examining the toxic relational strategies that we were subject to as well as ones we have subjected others to. Paying attention to the bidirectional flow of these patterns is the first step in true change.

This list is based on research and training materials from multiple sources including the Safer Society Foundation, the University of Iowa, Moral Reconation Therapy, and Faith's office partner (work wife) Brenda Martinez, who is a trauma-informed licensed professional counselor and licensed sex offender treatment provider. It is not intended to represent the totality of toxic relational patterns, but to start a conversation on how they affect your own life.

Anger as Means of Control: When we use anger to control and manipulate the behavior of others. The difference between this kind of anger and impulsive anger is that the anger response is turned off the minute we get what we want.

Employed by: ◯ Self ◯ Family of Origin ◯ Past Relationships ◯ Current Relationships

Authoritarian Dominance: When we hold rigid boundaries and expectations that things be done "our" way.

Employed by: ◯ Self ◯ Family of Origin ◯ Past Relationships ◯ Current Relationships

Belittling: When we treat others (or their feelings, concerns, point of view) as comparatively unimportant.

Employed by: ◯ Self ◯ Family of Origin ◯ Past Relationships ◯ Current Relationships

Black and White Decreeing: When we term everything in extremes ("I can never trust women," or "All men are players.")

Employed by: ◯ Self ◯ Family of Origin ◯ Past Relationships ◯ Current Relationships

Blaming: When we place blame elsewhere or insist that others are responsible for our behavior. Also could be termed a **refusal to accept responsibility.**

Employed by: ◯ Self ◯ Family of Origin ◯ Past Relationships ◯ Current Relationships

Compartmentalization of Behavior: When we compartmentalize our behavior to keep from feeling guilty, to justify our actions, or minimize the seriousness of them. ("I only cheat when out of town for work, never when I'm home")

Employed by: ◯ Self ◯ Family of Origin ◯ Past Relationships ◯ Current Relationships

Credit Seeking: When we want credit for good behavior (Okay, I forgot to pay the electric bill and the power was turned off, but don't I get credit for paying the water bill and the Netflix?) or credit for extremes not engaged in (Okay, I wrecked your car...but I could have lied about it and said someone rammed into it while I was at the grocery store) rather than accepting accountability for behavior in question.

Employed by: ◯ Self ◯ Family of Origin ◯ Past Relationships ◯ Current Relationships

Criminal Pride: Feeling a sense of identity and accomplishment from hurting others, e.g. "This is just how I am" or "This is just how I grew up."

Employed by: ⬭ Self ⬭ Family of Origin ⬭ Past Relationships ⬭ Current Relationships

Diverting: When we change the subject to something more comfortable, intentionally redirect the conversation, bring up another problem, or intentionally miss the point of the conversation at hand.

Employed by: ⬭ Self ⬭ Family of Origin ⬭ Past Relationships ⬭ Current Relationships

Entitlement: When we think someone owes us something or the world owes us something because we are special, different, or have been through more than others have.

Employed by: ⬭ Self ⬭ Family of Origin ⬭ Past Relationships ⬭ Current Relationships

Fact Stacking: When we arrange facts in a way to explain our behavior, while omitting other facts that don't work in our favor.

Employed by: ⬭ Self ⬭ Family of Origin ⬭ Past Relationships ⬭ Current Relationships

Fairness Violation: When we believe that everyone is treating us unfairly and/or when we keep a mental scorecard regarding "fairness" in the relationship.

Employed by: ⬭ Self ⬭ Family of Origin ⬭ Past Relationships ⬭ Current Relationships

Fight Instigating: When we encourage others to fight, then we stand back and watch.

Employed by: ⬭ Self ⬭ Family of Origin ⬭ Past Relationships ⬭ Current Relationships

Frequency Minimization: When we minimize the behavior based on frequency (It didn't happen five times, it was three times at most!). This is a form of **playing defense attorney.**

Employed by: ⬭ Self ⬭ Family of Origin ⬭ Past Relationships ⬭ Current Relationships

Gaslighting: When we deliberately obscure or twist facts to make others question their reality, memory, and ultimate sanity.

Employed by: ⬭ Self ⬭ Family of Origin ⬭ Past Relationships ⬭ Current Relationships

Grandiosity: When we make little things into huge, important things so we can shift the focus of attention.

Employed by: ◯ Self ◯ Family of Origin ◯ Past Relationships ◯ Current Relationships

Harm Discounting: When we insist that our actions did not cause the level of harm that others say they did ("I did it, but it is certainly not as bad as you think."). This is another form of **playing defense attorney.**

Employed by: ◯ Self ◯ Family of Origin ◯ Past Relationships ◯ Current Relationships

Helplessness: When we act incapable or helpless and unable to do things for ourselves, needing others to do them for us.

Employed by: ◯ Self ◯ Family of Origin ◯ Past Relationships ◯ Current Relationships

Impulsiveness: When we can't wait for what we want and do not want to delay our desires, and pursue these desires at the expense of others.

Employed by: ◯ Self ◯ Family of Origin ◯ Past Relationships ◯ Current Relationships

Intention Denial: When we deny our intention for harm. It may be true that we didn't intend to be hurtful or didn't plan a way to control someone else, but that doesn't lessen the impact of our behavior and it is another way of diminishing our responsibility for our actions. ("I didn't mean it" or "Things just got out of control.")

Employed by: ◯ Self ◯ Family of Origin ◯ Past Relationships ◯ Current Relationships

Justice Seeking: When we punish or control others and frame it as punitive toward others because of their behavior toward us. This is another form of **playing defense attorney.**

Employed by: ◯ Self ◯ Family of Origin ◯ Past Relationships ◯ Current Relationships

Justifying: When we justify our behavior so we don't have to take responsibility ("I wouldn't have hit you if you hadn't made me so angry").

Employed by: ◯ Self ◯ Family of Origin ◯ Past Relationships ◯ Current Relationships

Keeping Score: When we explain or **justify** behavior based on the past actions of others or ourselves ("I've always done more than you, so it's not a big deal that I didn't do what I said I would this week.")
Employed by: ◯ Self ◯ Family of Origin ◯ Past Relationships ◯ Current Relationships

Lying: When we intentionally state things that are not true, or do not include all details in an attempt to deceive.
Employed by: ◯ Self ◯ Family of Origin ◯ Past Relationships ◯ Current Relationships

Making Excuses: Similar to **justifying**, in that we use it to explain away our behavior rather than hold ourselves accountable ("I was depressed that day.")
Employed by: ◯ Self ◯ Family of Origin ◯ Past Relationships ◯ Current Relationships

Making Fools of: When we exaggerate the mistakes and weaknesses of others to intentionally demean them and lessen their voice and authority.
Employed by: ◯ Self ◯ Family of Origin ◯ Past Relationships ◯ Current Relationships

Minimizing: When we try to make a behavior seem like it has less impact on those around us ("At least I only made out with them and didn't sleep with them.")
Employed by: ◯ Self ◯ Family of Origin ◯ Past Relationships ◯ Current Relationships

Mind Reading: When we think we know what other people are thinking and make decisions based on these assumptions, rather than asking.
Employed by: ◯ Self ◯ Family of Origin ◯ Past Relationships ◯ Current Relationships

Ownership: When we feel a sense of ownership of other people, and feel entitled to control their behavior.
Employed by: ◯ Self ◯ Family of Origin ◯ Past Relationships ◯ Current Relationships

Phoniness: When we communicate and apologize insincerely, without fully taking responsibility and without intent to change (maybe just intending to stop getting caught).
Employed by: ◯ Self ◯ Family of Origin ◯ Past Relationships ◯ Current Relationships

Playing Dumb: When we act confused about a situation to avoid responsibility for our behavior, or continuously ask questions that imply we don't understand what others are communicating. ("What did I do? What's wrong with that? What do you mean by that?")

Employed by: ◯ Self ◯ Family of Origin ◯ Past Relationships ◯ Current Relationships

Projecting: When we presume what others are thinking, feeling, or doing based on what we are thinking, feeling, or doing.

Employed by: ◯ Self ◯ Family of Origin ◯ Past Relationships ◯ Current Relationships

Pushing Buttons: When we intentionally use information about another person to get them upset in order to distract from our behavior.

Employed by: ◯ Self ◯ Family of Origin ◯ Past Relationships ◯ Current Relationships

Secretive Behavior: When we hide our activities and omit information to keep people from knowing what we are doing.

Employed by: ◯ Self ◯ Family of Origin ◯ Past Relationships ◯ Current Relationships

Selfish Intent: When we think and act in terms of our needs only, and not the needs of others.

Employed by: ◯ Self ◯ Family of Origin ◯ Past Relationships ◯ Current Relationships

Self-Pitying: When we use statements decrying how bad we are in order to get attention paid to us ("No one cares about me" or "Everyone would be better off without me around")

Employed by: ◯ Self ◯ Family of Origin ◯ Past Relationships ◯ Current Relationships

Spiritual/Philosophical Bypassing: When we invoke religion or spirituality over personal responsibility in an attempt to ascribe different meaning to a situation or to avoid doing the work around uncomfortable emotions ("I'm just turning it over to God." Or "What does any of this mean at a constructivist level, anyway?")

Employed by: ◯ Self ◯ Family of Origin ◯ Past Relationships ◯ Current Relationships

Uniqueness: When we believe that we are unique in such a way that consideration of others (and sometimes rules and laws regarding conduct) do not apply to us in the same way.

Employed by: ◯ Self ◯ Family of Origin ◯ Past Relationships ◯ Current Relationships

Vagueness: When we respond vaguely or unclearly in order to distract from the truth or the content of the conversation.

Employed by: ◯ Self ◯ Family of Origin ◯ Past Relationships ◯ Current Relationships

Victimization Reversal: When we present ourselves as the victim in a scenario, rather than taking responsibility for our role in any events that occurred.

Employed by: ◯ Self ◯ Family of Origin ◯ Past Relationships ◯ Current Relationships

Wearing Down: When we continuously challenge others to give us what we want until they acquiesce out of exhaustion over the continued fighting.

Employed by: ◯ Self ◯ Family of Origin ◯ Past Relationships ◯ Current Relationships

Zero State: Feeling worthless, like nothing, a no-body, and/or empty inside and behaving in ways to help fill that void. This is often where narcissistic behavior stems from.

Employed by: ◯ Self ◯ Family of Origin ◯ Past Relationships ◯ Current Relationships

Questions to consider as you go through this list:

Did you notice any patterns in your answers? Do certain strategies come up time and again?

What strategies have you used on other people?

Do you use different strategies for different people (partners versus friends versus family, for example)?

What strategies were used against you in the past? By whom?

What strategies are being used against you in current relationships? By whom?

Are there any patterns that you notice in the strategies you use and the ones used against you?

Are there any patterns that you notice in the strategies that have been used against you in the past and are being used against you in current relationships?

What is one strategy that you have noticed in yourself that you want to commit to changing? How will you do so?

What is one strategy that you have noticed in your current relationships that you are committed to no longer accepting? How will you do so?

The Inventory: How To Stop Keeping Secrets From Yourself

In 12 step recovery, step 4 is a bear. It's the place that Faith has found to be the place where her clients are most likely to relapse. Which doesn't mean they should be skipped, but that a fuck-ton of support is generally in order. In Bill W. parlance, step 4 is "We make a searching and fearless moral inventory of ourselves." And Russell Brand, in his book *Recovery: Freedom From Our Addictions*, (which big recommend in case you are wondering) calls it ""Write down all the things that are fucking you up or have ever fucked you up, and don't lie or leave anything out." This inventory is a big excavation. You'll notice that much of the work in this section is about tools to help you stop keeping secrets from yourself and this is a big one. This version borrows heavily from the aforementioned Russell Brand book as well as the *Big Book Awakening: 12 Step Workbook*.

Firstly, you are going to use the following page to list out all the people in your life that you remember having interactions with. We're gonna do this in 5 year chunks (0-5, 5-10, etc until you get to your today years old number). This is a trick Russell Brand got from a mentor on how to do a relational timeline so no one was missed. Because we are working with times that are long ago and you were really young, you may not remember people's names. It may be someone who had enough influence in your life that you recollect them but their name has become memory dust. It's okay to list them in whatever way helps you remember. If your kindergarten teacher was Mrs. Meisenheimer (she was and she was a heinous bitch to me) but you don't remember her name calling her Crabface McGee, or whatever else floats your boat is also acceptable.

Do the list first and then go through it and mark the name of every person to whom you feel a sense of resentment. Biomom, stepbrother, that kid on the school bus, Crabface McGee herself. If it bubbles up, it's something you're carrying. Even if it was decades ago. Highlight them, put an asterisk by their name, whatever works best.

Age (eg, 0-5)	People I encountered

Now we are going to list out everyone on your "resentment list." That goes in column one. Column two is the space for the "because". So I resent Mrs. Meisenheimer because she shamed me for being left handed and having terrible writing in general.

Now we are going to go through every line on our resentment list and figure out how this resentment affected us, using the following ideas we have about ourselves (and about ourselves in relationship to others). To keep it simple, here are the main categories. For each resentment, list all that apply.

Self-Worth: How I think or feel about myself.

Self-in-Relation: How I think others see me or feel about me

Ambition: What I wanted to happen in this situation (a goal or plan I had for myself)

Security: What I needed to be safe, what I needed to be okay

Relational Images: My beliefs about how this relationship was supposed to be

Cultural Images: My beliefs about how individuals are supposed to interact in the world around them (based on their gender, age, status, etc.)

Financial: How my finances were impacted or how I thought they might be in the future.

I resent...	Because...	Category

Okay, now we are gonna choose the biggest resentments and look at our part in them. This is our inventory, not Mrs. Meisenheimer's right? We are going to look at our part in each resentment, either in the moment that it occurred or how we carried it forward. We have room to get you started here, but if you're carrying around more baggage than fits in these worksheets, feel free to do more in a notebook.

Resentment #1: _____

What mistakes am I responsible for in this dynamic?

In what ways did I engage in selfish attitudes?

What self-seeking actions, behaviors, and activities did I engage in?

What lies did I tell myself about this situation?

What fears drove these lies?

What harms did I perpetuate?

Resentment #2: _____

What mistakes am I responsible for in this dynamic?

In what ways did I engage in selfish attitudes?

What self-seeking actions, behaviors, and activities did I engage in?

What lies did I tell myself about this situation?

What fears drove these lies?

What harms did I perpetuate?

Resentment #3: _____

What mistakes am I responsible for in this dynamic?

In what ways did I engage in selfish attitudes?

What self-seeking actions, behaviors, and activities did I engage in?

What lies did I tell myself about this situation?

What fears drove these lies?

What harms did I perpetuate?

Resentment #4: _____

What mistakes am I responsible for in this dynamic?

In what ways did I engage in selfish attitudes?

What self-seeking actions, behaviors, and activities did I engage in?

What lies did I tell myself about this situation?

What fears drove these lies?

What harms did I perpetuate?

Shadow Work

The "shadow" is a concept in Jungian psychology that is complicated but essentially means the part of our psyche that we consider negative and undesirable. But this part functions as part of a greater whole. Everyone has a shadow side and we need that to be a complete person. When we can really see and respect that part of ourselves, it doesn't make us evil, it makes us less likely to do destructive behaviors, have better boundaries, relationships, and communication skills, and even improves our physical health..

So how does one "do" shadow work? It's self-reflection work, which means journaling, meditation, and other means of processing. (Jung also thought that using concepts of archetypes can be helpful to shadow work but that's a worksheet of a different color.)

It's really important to have some good grounding skills before starting shadow work in your mental health toolkit (like the STOP or TIPP skills at the beginning of this workbook or anything else you have in your healthy self-care toolbox). Shadow work is difficult and really activating, so having ways to stay safe in your body is really important.

Shadow Work Questions for Introspection

What kinds of emotions do you try to avoid?

What kinds of people do you try to avoid?

What dreams have you had that upset you the most? What happened within them?

If you could erase one memory what would it be?

What do you not like about yourself?

What makes you feel the most insecure?

What aspects of your life are most disconcerting to you?

What kinds of issues are you most likely to hold grudges about?

What have you held a grudge about the longest?

Which kinds of irrational fears are most likely to hold you back?

Which irrational fear has been the biggest barrier to you recently?

What are your bad habits?

What prevents you from "breaking" them?

What kinds of lies do you tell yourself?

In what ways are you regularly hypocritical?

What is the biggest promise you've made to yourself that you broke?

What relationships do you hold on to that are unhealthy?

In what other ways do you self-sabotage?

Shadow Work Meditation

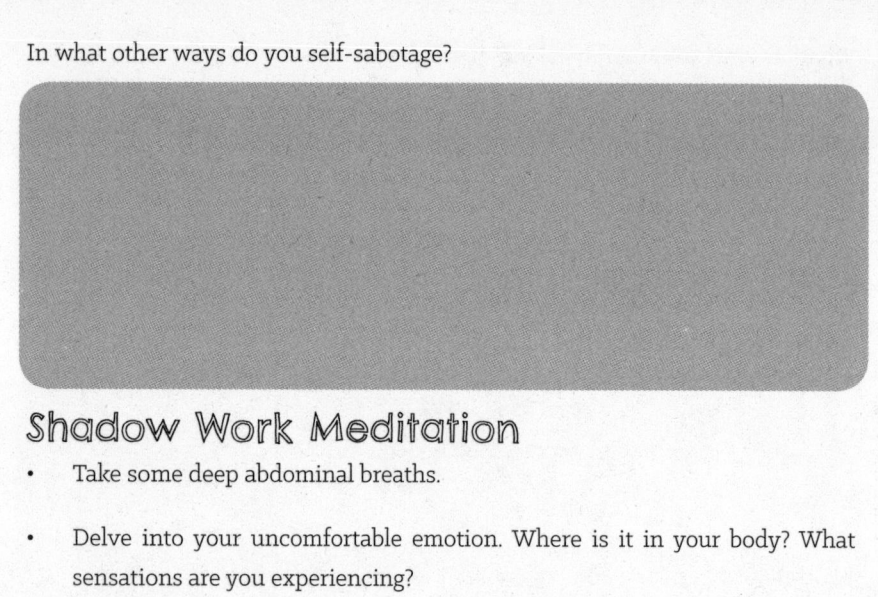

- Take some deep abdominal breaths.

- Delve into your uncomfortable emotion. Where is it in your body? What sensations are you experiencing?

- Ask yourself, "What are these emotions and sensations trying to teach me? What do I need to understand about this situation?"

- Let your sensations and emotions move and shift. Notice what they do with curiosity instead of judgement.

- Jot down any observations you made or insights you had.

Shadow Work Self-Check-In

Now, take a moment to consider a few experiences from your life in the context of your shadow self.

Why do you think you have had trouble accepting accountability for outcomes in the past?

What is the worst consequence you recall experiencing when you did accept responsibility for a negative outcome?

What was the worst consequence you've faced when you did not accept responsibility?

For what past error or failure have you not accepted responsibility? Can you take action to correct that neglect or intentional rejection of acknowledging your accountability?

When do you find it easiest to express your feelings?

What is the biggest risk you've ever taken?

When did you feel most overextended?

What causes you to act defensively? How would you like to respond instead?

Where do you feel safest? Why?

How have you changed in the past year? Why?

What is empathy? Why is it important to you?

How can you be a better listener?

How can you support people that you've hurt?

What is your definition of justice?

How can you be transparent about your progress?

What has been the most transformative experience in your life to date? How did it happen? What was meaningful about it?

WHAT SHOULD I DO NEXT?

1. **WRITE** down all of your goals.
2. Break these goals down into **ACTIONABLE TASKS**.
3. Identify all of the tasks that will take less than **FIVE MINUTES**. DO THEM NOW.
4. Ask stakeholders for **DEADLINES** and to assign a priority of 0-10 to each task.
5. Add up the **TOTAL PRIORITY** for each task, based on the priority that your stakeholders place on it.
6. **EVALUATE** how many hours each step should take. You will get this wrong at first. That's okay.
7. Determine which steps you can **DELEGATE**.
8. **SCHEDULE** each part of the highest priority tasks onto your calendar before the deadline.
9. If you cannot complete something on schedule, **COMMUNICATE** to the stakeholders what you can deliver when.
10. Start on the **HIGHEST PRIORITY** task with the soonest deadline.
11. If you are having trouble getting started, break each task into further **ACTIONABLE STEPS**.
12. Review your **TO-DO LIST** for five minutes at the end of every day to prepare your work for the following day.
13. When you remember something else or more work is assigned, stop and immediately **ADD IT TO YOUR LIST**.
14. When you finish something difficult or time-consuming, **REWARD YOURSELF** with something tasty or fun.
15. When you are overwhelmed by the size of your to-do list, step back and **REMOVE THINGS** that are no longer needed.
16. When in doubt, ask yourself is this an **EMERGENCY OR PRIORITY**. If not, it shouldn't be your next task.
17. **PRACTICE SIMPLIFYING** this list weekly.
18. When in doubt, ask the person overseeing you to create a list of **DESCENDING PRIORITIES** for you.
19. Remember that if you are lacking time, money, or capacity, you can **ADAPT YOUR APPROACH** and focus more on the other two to make up for it.
20. If you can, **AUTOMATE** a task. If it isn't priority, you can **ELIMINATE** a task or find a way to **DELEGATE**.

TROUBLESHOOTING

Unclear About GOALS? Consider how your work supports others and see step 17.

Don't Understand WHY YOU'RE DOING A TASK? Ask the stakeholders to take you from the trees to see the forest.

Not PERSONALLY INVESTED? Delegate or seek more information to make each task meaningful for you.

UNDERMOTIVATED? Evaluate what makes you care deeply. Talk to other people on your team to get excited about your shared goals.

OVERWHELMED? Consider easier paths. Go to steps 10, 12, 16, and 17. Please be kind to yourself.

Worried About Your PERFORMANCE? Ask your stakeholders for their expectations.

HUNGRY? THIRSTY? LOW BLOOD SUGAR? Take a break to take care of yourself. You'll do better work.

Are you ANXIOUS? Focus on a smaller task instead to get your confidence up.

FEELINGS OVERRIDING YOUR Judgment? Think about your team and goals and how success will make life easier even if it's difficult.

© Joe Biel, 2019, JoeBiel.net. This poster and other infographics like it are available from www.Microcosm.Pub
For more help getting your tasks done, check out Jessie Kwak's *From Chaos to Creativity*

Barriers to Accountability

Remember how accountability is shedding all of your inherited baggage and making your own choices for what's best for you? Well, you probably cannot remind yourself of that too often. And it's easier said than done.

In 2010 Internet activist Eli Pariser coined the term "filter bubble" to describe the way that only selective information can penetrate our social groups. When we traffick the Internet, what is shown to us is based on our previous activities. Soon this creates a closed loop as only information reinforcing our views is introduced. Our ability to become more educated and informed is actively undermined by these engines telling us what they think we want to hear and preventing information that conflicts with our views from reaching us.

Have you ever noticed that it's easy to generalize or stigmatize someone for a single action while we can justify doing the exact same thing? If someone else runs a stop sign, they are a "bad driver." If we do the same thing, we are "in a hurry to do an important favor for a sick friend."

Most of our behavior is coded and hardwired. Our brain remembers to take a shower after we wake up and then eat breakfast. We salivate and build upon needed chemicals to perform these tasks on a schedule. So imagine how difficult and confusing it can be for our brains when you are changing behavior, when you are becoming accountable. It's not your fault. You just have to remember that your brain is under construction and might take a little while to figure out what you are up to.

On a bigger scale, you may have heard the troubling and defeatist phrase "an abused child becomes a childish abusive adult" or "hurt people hurt people." However, these ideologies, like most ideologies, only represent part of the reality of an abusive childhood.

First, abused children develop maladaptive coping mechanisms to attempt to get their needs met. A hungry child might steal from the corner store if their parents don't provide for them[2]. They understand that they are harming others but they need to eat. They may also have siblings that need to eat. They recognize that telling other adults about their household will get people in trouble, so they resolve the issue and protect the only family system they know. As they age into adulthood, those habits may remain even after they are unnecessary.

Second, a traumatized person feels shame in their trauma. The shame tells them that the trauma is their fault. Shame tells us we are a mistake, not a person who made mistakes. If you stole to feed your family, you didn't "do what was necessary out of desperation," you are a thief, presumably because you have no morals, values, ethics, or concern for others. Trauma often plays out in the person not feeling taken seriously and going to extreme lengths to make their case, often by exaggerating. We replay and echo these voices in our own heads, even if no one has ever explicitly said these things to us. We know the worst light in which our actions can be cast and we are often quite ready to see ourselves in this unflattering way.

If we have the perception that we never exercise, it reduces our motivation for following through in the present and future. When we crave chocolate, we don't necessarily contemplate if it's healthy, when we had it last, or why we want it so badly. We justify our need for it and why we deserve it. Conversely, if every attempt to talk about our feelings with our parents was met with annoyance and dismissal, we won't talk to our loved ones about how we feel, even if they desperately want to hear it.

In psychology, these prior experiences (priors), values, and attitudes shape and sometimes distort our present reasoning. This is termed the belief-bias effect, and it frames our lived experiences and strengthens our subconscious decision-making considerations. They can also lead us to some spectacular leaps in logic.

Have you ever noticed that it's easy to generalize or stigmatize someone for a single action while we can justify doing the exact same thing? If someone else runs a stop sign, they are a "bad driver." If we do the same thing, we are "in a hurry to do an important favor for a sick friend."

---

[2] Oppositional defiant disorder is correlated most strongly with poverty than any other identifier about a child.

Fortunately, there are ways to rewire our brain, overcome these barriers, and change behaviors. When we recognize ourselves as out of alignment, and choose to do the difficult work of accountability, we must first get to a deeper understanding of how we fell out of alignment to begin with. Why do we have behavioral grooves that don't align with our values, goals, or sometimes even with our own best interests? It's typically because of some combination of trauma reactions, heuristics and biases, thinking errors, and relationship paradigms. To understand how this works, we need to understand how our brains work, both alone and in groups. Accountability involves not just saying sorry for past actions but understanding how cognitive shortcuts create problematic patterns of behavior, and by recognizing this we can avoid repeating them in the present.

Thinking Errors

Just like cognitive biases, we each tend to make mistakes in our thinking that can cause no end of problems in our approaches and relationships, and can become barriers to our accountability. The list below is only partial—you can find many more online.

We all do all of these at some point. It's how our brains are wired to work. For each one, note a situation where you believe you may have been operating from a thinking error. And check the box next to the ones you struggle with on the regular.

☐ **Filtering**: Filtering happens when you pick out the one damn negative and don't look at anything else from the situation that is either positive or just neutral. Faith is a professional trainer. You better believe Faith can teach 50 people and get 49 superlative reviews but perseverate on the one review that bitches about her potty mouth (fuck yeah!). With filtering, you are not including any context, because you are isolating what you are focusing on from the circumstances around it. Which means it becomes the entirety of your focus rather than just a percentage of your information.

A time I have done this:

☐ **Polarized Thinking**: This is as black and white as a yin-yang symbol. Everything gets categorized as either good or bad. Then there is no middle ground. Which means if you aren't completely perfect, you must be a total failure.

A time I have done this:

☐ **Overgeneralization**: This takes the polarized thinking to a whole new level. It's your brain taking one example of something that happened one time and deciding this is how things are going to roll forever. So if you failed at something, you are a failure and will continue to be so for time eternal. So why even bother trying?

A time I have done this:

☐ **Mind Reading**: This is where you decide you know without a doubt why people are acting the way they act, saying what they say, and what they are thinking and feeling. Huge-ass leaps to conclusions. This is a lot of times based on projection. We know how we are thinking and feeling and presume that others would think and feel the same. Or we feel so shitty about ourselves that we presume others must have the same opinion of us. Someone didn't notice you? They totally must hate you, according to your brain. When, in reality, they are focused on why George R.R. Martin won't finish the damn Game of Thrones series or something that has nothing to do with you in that moment.

A time I have done this:

☐ **Personalization**: So we all have the tendency to be the star of our own personal movie, right? And if we are the star, then everything going on around us must relate to us, right? So we are mind reading other people's intent as being about us instead of about them and presume that the ways they respond are due to something negative about us.

A time I have done this:

☐ **Control Fallacies**: Fallacies of control fuck you up in either direction. If you feel totally controlled by everything around you, then you are totally a helpless victim. If you feel that you have to be in control of everything all the time, you feel responsible for everything all of the time. Neither is an empirical truth. Both extremes set you up for failure and exhaustion.

A time I have done this:

☐ **Fallacy of Fairness**: I was pretty damn young when my mom told me, in essence, that life wasn't fair and I was exhausting myself by expecting it to be. If you are keeping a running fairness tally, you are going to be resentful to pissed off all the time.

A time I have done this:

☐ **Blaming**: This is where you blame other people for the pain you feel and the problems you have. Now, people may fuck you over big time, but blaming them for everything that comes after means making them responsible for all of your choices and decisions for time eternal. That's far too much power to give over to some motherfucker. In reality, you have every right to be your own self-advocate, to make your own choices and be responsible for your own decisions from here on out.

A time I have done this:

☐ **Shoulds**: Dude. If people would just do what I say, the world would be a brilliant place. We all have a list of shoulds for the rest of the world. How people should behave. How they should treat us. When they don't follow those rules, we get all kinds of legit butthurt. Then we put on our judgy-pants about what they are doing, even when it's shit that we seriously don't even need to be worrying about.

A time I have done this:

☐ **Emotional Reasoning**: This is where we presume that whatever emotion we are feeling is an indicator of something fucked up about ourselves. That if we feel something, it must be a fundamental truth. Like, if you feel guilty, you clearly are guilty. And while feelings are real, they don't always correspond to reality. If our thinking is distorted, then our emotional reactions go along for the ride and it becomes a mobius strip of mind-fuckery.

A time I have done this:

☐ **Fallacy of Change**: This is the expectation that people should change to make life better for you. And that their changing is what is going to make you happy. Of course you can always ask people to change. But the only person you can really control is your own damn self. And the choices you make will have far more of an impact on your happiness, because then you can take credit for successes.

A time I have done this:

☐ **Global Labeling**: This is the shitty political extremist category of distorted thinking styles. It's all about stereotyping and one-dimensionality, as if knowing one thing allows you to know everything. It's what leads to prejudice, relationship issues, and the tendency to make snap judgments. For example, there is some dude in front of you in line at the store wearing a camo ball cap. Global labeling might mean automatically presuming he's a racist redneck just because you noticed the hat, but without having any other information about the dude.

A time I have done this:

☐ **Being Right**: You feel like you have something to prove in every interaction . . . and what you need to prove is your inherent rightness. You are lawyer, judge, and jury . . . and you aren't hearing anything from the opposition. A different opinion or perspective? INADMISSIBLE! Being right can really fuck up your ability to have caring and reciprocal relationships with others.

A time I have done this:

☐ **Heaven's Reward Fallacy**: Heaven's Reward folks totally went to church with grandma. They are the people who have some kind of sense that if they deny themselves and sacrifice constantly, they are somehow working toward some magical reward because there is a scorecard being kept. This isn't about people who are trying to be better human beings, because that's what we should all do, but a sort of false piety that speaks to paying into the system like it's an investment. Then, of course, when the reward doesn't come (because it doesn't have to be a literal storing of your treasures in heaven; maybe you are expecting public recognition of your moral superiority) it sucks pretty bad and creates serious bitterness. What was all the sacrifice for, then? If you aren't doing the right thing with your heart truly in it, you're just depleting yourself without real payoff.

A time I have done this:

Cognitive Biases

Because of how human brains work, we have biases. We can become stuck in patterns of stereotyping and prejudicial thinking. We can fail to take in additional information, recognize situational context, or think beyond that well-tread neural pathway. There's a whole chapter about this in the accompanying book.

If you do a google search, you can find as many different lists of cognitive biases as there are types of tacos, so for the sake of our work here we're going to stick with the ten common ones that are most supported by the original research conducted by Amos Tversky and Daniel Kahneman in 1972 on heuristics and biases.

Just being aware of our biases makes us almost 30% less likely to react to them. Additional bias management tools (including attending to multiple factors and challenging our internal thought patterns) are something we are going to delve into more deeply later in this book. There is even a whole therapeutic modality, known as cognitive bias modification therapy, that has tricks and tips we can all use in our day to day lives to avoid these little logical pitfalls.

Since these are all pretty universal human experiences, use the space after each bias to write an example of a situation where you can recognize you may have been operating from this particular bias. Check the box next to each bias that you notice gets you into trouble fairly frequently.

☐ **Actor-Observer Bias**: Our likelihood of attributing our own behavior to external causes, while attributing other people's behavior to internal causes. For example, if I cut someone off in traffic it was because I couldn't see them in my blind spot, but if someone cuts me off it's because they're a dickhead.

A time I have done this:

☐ **Anchoring Bias**: Our likelihood of relying too heavily on the first piece of information we learn. Faith was horrified to find out how much a car battery cost a few years ago, presuming it would be close to the $60 she paid for one the first time in 1996. In the same way, racist, phobic, and ableist trash ideas fed to someone as a child can become an anchoring bias they carry into adulthood.

A time I have done this:

☐ **Attentional Bias**: Our inclination to include certain information while ignoring other information. The number of people who have been fooled by "cauliflower pizza crust" because they didn't notice that the crust was mostly rice flour and therefore just as carb heavy as something from Dominoes is not a small number.

A time I have done this:

☐ **Availability Bias**: The availability bias is a direct function of the availability heuristic mentioned above, it refers to our likelihood of believing something just because the idea is readily available. Just like Faith's most recent car break-in was easier to refer back to than the one that happened in front of her house many years ago, it was easier for her to worry more about Guadalupe street than her own subdivision.

A time I have done this:

☐ **Confirmation Bias**: When we seek out data that supports what we already believe and discount the information that challenges it. When you are researching a topic, you are more likely to believe the article that most closely aligns with your already held views. If you think Politician X is a liar, you're going to presume things they say are falsehoods and disregard anything that demonstrates the veracity of their statements. (And a not-so-slight aside? Our social media feeds have algorithms that directly play into these confirmation biases which makes them even stronger and more difficult to uproot).

A time I have done this:

☐ **Dunning-Kruger Effect Bias**: The bias we have at thinking we are better at something than we actually are. Interestingly, this seems tied to whether or not we rehearse something in our minds. This applies to everything from logical reasoning to assuming that a professional job would be easy for us. Without experience and competence from doing something, we can't recognize our own lack of skill. It makes us think we can do it in real life since we "storied" it. It's not just pure ego, it's a definite brain quirk.

A time I have done this:

☐ **False Consensus Bias**: What happens when we tend to overestimate the number of people who agree with you. Faith experiences this every damn time there is a local election. She is always heartwarmed to find that Facebook is filled with passionate and politically involved friends who vote, so she anticipates high numbers of participation. Then, invariably, she sees that, once again, voter turnout continues to be abysmal and that she is bumping into this bias.

A time I have done this:

☐ **Functional Fixedness Bias**: This is when we see things as working only in a particular way. Humans do this far more often than other animals who use tools, probably because we create stories (heuristics) about what that tool is meant to do, so we miss out on all the other things that it can do. Faith leaves a cast iron comal on her stove at all time (because she lives in San Antonio and tortillas are life), but recently found herself pulling out a frying pan to grill a little spaghetti squash rather than just toss it on the comal that was already available. I would like to point out (brag) that autistic people suffer from this much less, on the whole, and tend to implement tools in ways that the designers never foresaw.

A time I have done this:

☐ **Halo Effect Bias**: When our overall impression of a person affects what we think about their character or abilities. This is why we are more likely to believe the best of someone we find attractive and why people we find attractive tend to make more money than those of us who are squishy and average looking.

A time I have done this:

☐ **Misinformation Effect Bias**: This refers to the brain's tendency to confabulate and misremember details, and even believe we had the direct experience of something because we heard someone else did. This is why eyewitness testimony is actually fairly unreliable.

A time I have done this:

☐ **Optimism Bias**: We tend to expect that we are less likely to experience misfortune than someone else. Which is why so many people will continue bad health habits even as they see those around them fall sick.

A time I have done this:

☐ **Self-Serving Bias**: This is an internal versus external locus of control error again, much like the Actor-Observer Bias. In this case, it's about the outcome. We are much more likely to see good fortune as something we earned while thinking others lucked into it.

A time I have done this:

How to Make a Decision

What is my desired outcome?

What is the simplest solution to achieve it? Is there an easier way?

Does my idea work for everybody involved? Y / N STOP / GO

Are the costs & consequences acceptable? Y / N STOP / GO

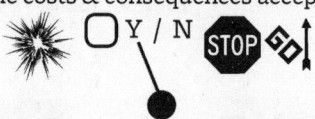

What are the worst, best, and likely outcomes? Can I manage them all? Y / N STOP / GO

Does this decision cause harm to anyone I care about and/or our relationship? STOP / GO Y / N

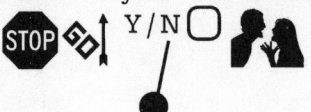

Does this decision take too much time and energy from the things I want and need to do? STOP / GO Y / N

Could this decision cost more money than I can afford? Is there a cheaper way? STOP / GO Y / N

DO IT!

Change Your Behavior

Now that you've done a fuck ton of work getting to know yourself and why you do the things you do— great work on that—it's time to get down to the behavior change part. It might not even be as straightforward as you previously thought, but there are tricks and formulas.

Resmaa Menakem, in his book My Grandmother's Hands, differentiate types of pain as either dirty or clean. This relates to the classic idea of Buddhist philosophy that pain is inevitable but suffering is optional. The pain doesn't change, but our relationship with it does. . . and we can use it to progress as human beings. Resmaa defines dirty pain as "the pain of avoidance, blame, and denial" and clean pain as "pain that mends and can build your capacity for growth."

Doing the work of self-reflection, and behavioral change, is the transformative work of clean pain. But what does that look like in practice?

How do we avoid making the same mistakes over and over again in terms of biased thinking, trauma responsive behavior, and the like? Good old fashioned habit formation. But maybe you are thinking, "Hey, fuckers. I've already tried to build better habits and failed often and epically enough that I am reading your book so you can help me the fuck out."

Don't worry, we are still gonna help you the fuck out.

Self-Compassion

Self-compassion means recognizing our own suffering with kindness and empathy, just the way we might feel for a friend who is hurting, and working to ease that suffering. This is different from self-esteem, which hinges on external events.

The three original components of self-compassion, defined by Kristen Neff, are: self-kindness, common humanity, and mindfulness. When I talk about it, I add a fourth one, self-empathy. This term and the definition comes from psychologist and mediator Marshall Rosenberg's work on non-violent communication.

Mindfulness: Awareness of our current experience. Literally what is going on inside you in the present—all of your thoughts, feelings, and sensations. Without trying to suppress it or control it or judge it. Just saying "Oh hey. There you are."

What are you thinking and feeling right now?

Self-Empathy: With mindfulness, we are tuning in to all of our internal experiences. Self-empathy is an inner questioning of the core inner experience to which we are the most attuned. This one is about allowing ourselves to be curious, and asking "What is at the heart of this feeling?"

What core need has been driving your current thoughts and feelings? You can refer back to the Needs list earlier in the book.

Self-Kindness: This means being tender with ourselves, rather than shitty and judgmental about our failings. Compassionate self-kindness is something we do in the presence of pain. If you cut your hand, even doing something dumb, you would go clean it off and bandage it, right? We do this with our physical selves, but rarely with our emotional selves. Self-kindness is the cleaning and caring of the wound so it can heal.

What is the kindest thing you can do for yourself or say to yourself right now?

Common Humanity: This means simply, recognizing, "Wow yeah, I'm human, and I'm hurting, and other people feel this way too…we're all part of it." It's a realization that I am not alone in my pain and imperfection and do not have to isolate myself in this process. I am experiencing something that all human beings experience because we are all fucking human.

How does your self-criticism impact your relationship with others?

When Presented with New Information

We know we have biases. We know we have socia-centric and ego-centric behaviors. So we need to then challenge our self-determination of right-ness with a level of precision. Let's talk about the nine universal intellectual standards. Think of this as the terms and conditions of critical thinking before you click "subscribe" in your brain. For each standard, think of something you believe in passionately and list a time when you have successfully (or unsuccessfully) thought critically about it despite your emotional investment.

Clarity: What kind of elaboration would help you better understand the topic? Are there any examples of illustrations that can be used?

Accuracy: Is this verifiably free from errors or distortions? Did I check?

Precision: Is there an appropriate level of detail and specificity to this?

Relevance: Does this information bear directly on the issue at hand?

Depth: What other variables and complexities might be relevant?

Breadth: Is this viewpoint comprehensive? Have the views of others been taken into account?

Logic: Does this all fit together logically without contradictions?

Fairness: Is this free from bias, favoritism, and injustice?

Significance: Does this even fucking matter?

First Thought, Second Thought

Choosing how you respond to your feelings is easier said than done. One of the best things you can do is start capturing the beginning of the process. Rather than your automatic thoughts happening too quickly to notice, practice being aware of them. They are the chatter that bubbles up constantly and continuously in our dumb-ass brains. But if we just let our underlying brain chatter wander around unleashed, it will 100% shit the bed pretty quickly.

We're going to say it again because it's important: you aren't responsible for your first thought (that's the automatic one), but you are responsible for your second thought and your first behavior (that's the part you have control over). But to gain this control, you first have to recognize the initial thought so you can then tell yourself "That's utter crap, I'm not responding to that nonsense." Hopefully, the second thought can lead you into healthier behavior.

Think about a situation that was difficult for you recently. If it's one that you are working on accountability-wise that's great, but it could be anything that was uncomfortable or generally negative.

Describe the situation briefly

What automatic thoughts bubbled up for you while thinking about that?

What feelings did you experience?

What sensations?

Now check in with any thinking traps that you got caught up in based on these thoughts. You can refer to the lists of biases and thinking errors earlier. Notice any patterns?

Okay, so once we start seeing patterns in our automatic thoughts (and yes, I know, ugh….why did we ask you to look at that, they're horrible and depressing and that's apparently what's going on up there all day?) we can start to do the deeper work of figuring out how they have been feeding into our intermediate thoughts and our core beliefs. One of the best tricks for this is called the vertical arrow. The idea is we start distilling down the patterns in our automatic thoughts by questioning the meaning we have ascribed to them by challenging them. A simplified version of this technique could look something like this:

> If that's true, what would that mean?
>
> "It would mean I'm going to get fired."
>
> If that's true, what would that mean?
>
> "It would mean I won't be able to pay my bills and I will be homeless"
>
> If that's true, what would that mean?
>
> "It would mean I can't do anything right, and I'm a totally dysfunctional human"

But we can work with our stuck thoughts with even more elaboration. Challenge your automatic thoughts about the situation above with the following questions. Eventually this line of questioning should lead to the negative core belief. Core beliefs are internal "I" statements, like "I am" or "I can('t)." And in this case, we are looking for negative core beliefs that fall into three general categories:

- Helplessness
- Unlovability
- Worthlessness

Unpacking how our own thinking patterns are perpetuating continued mental health issues for us that then lead to destructive behavior is one of the first steps of true accountability work since we are training ourselves to watch our own tendencies and manage them in ways that are proactive rather than reactive.

First thought:

If that were true, what would that mean?

What would be the worst thing about this thought if it is true?

If that were true, what does that say about you?

If that were true, what does that say about others?

If that's true, what's the worst thing that could happen?

If that's true, what would that mean for the future?

Core negative belief:

Now let's look at a second thought. That is, what is a more helpful way of looking at the situation than the negative core belief that is driving your decision making process. Even if that first thought is somewhat accurate, it's not going to be a good mechanism for being your best self. What is a better lens on the situation?

Second thought:

Now, if you are operating from that second thought, what action would make the most sense to take. How would you behave from the second thought instead of the first?

Cognitive Defusion

A lot of our negative thoughts and feelings can come from internal judgments of ourselves that we may not even notice ourselves believing. One of the best tools from Acceptance and Commitment Therapy reframes our emotional responses through a technique called defusion. Defusion is the process of recognizing our thoughts and feelings as something we have rather than something that we are. Let's try it with some of the main critical meta-messages you have held about yourself:

My mind tells me I am too much of _____

My mind tells me I am not enough of _____

My mind tells me I do too much of _____

My mind tells me I do not do enough of _____

My mind tells me I lack _____

Now take this list and sit with it for a half a minute or so as something you are. Write it down, and even say out loud to yourself:

I am too awkward.

I am too lazy.

I don't move fast enough.

I am not _____

I am too _____

I lack _____

I can't _____

I shouldn't _____

Check in with yourself. How do you feel in your body after just half a minute of taking ownership of these thoughts?

Now try a shift out of judgement, by labeling it as a thought that exists, not something that you are.

I'm noticing that I'm having a thought about being too awkward.

I'm noticing that I am having a thought about being lazy.

I'm noticing that I am having a thought that I do not move fast enough.

I'm noticing that I am having a thought about being _____

I'm noticing that I am having a thought about not being _____

I'm noticing that I am having a thought about being too _____

I'm noticing that I am having a thought about not being able to _____

_____

I'm noticing that I am having a thought about _____

I'm noticing that I am having a thought about _____

I'm noticing that I am having a thought about _____

All defusion means (and yeah, sorry for the term . . . we like to create words for concepts to confuse as many people as possible) is that you are separating your self-ness out of your thoughts and noticing them as something that exists rather than something you are.

Check in with yourself again. How does your body feel when you are no longer fused with these thoughts as indicative of your self-hood?

Compassionate Accountability

Accountability is not self-hatred, self-blame, self-recrimination, or self-flagellation. It doesn't work that way, unless you really are one of the few literal billionaire "captains of industry," in which case go fuck yourself in the ear.

Buddhist theologians distinguish thusly between regret and shame. Regret is the ability to look at decisions and learn how not to repeat negative outcomes. Shame, on the other hand, internalizes behavior that we don't approve of and compels us to accept abhorrent behavior as part of our core personality; to accept our worst behavior as who we are. Brain science bears out this belief. Shame makes both a person's thinking and behavior inflexible as they believe that their behavior defines their character. We have this idea that in order to be better people, we have to be really hard on ourselves. We can't let ourselves off the hook right?

The problem with that gameplan (besides the fact that it's really shitty and mean) is that it doesn't work. Hard-assery doesn't work on ourselves or others, at least for long. It's exhausting, it's punitive, it's impossible to perfect so we end up backsliding into the crappy behavior that got us there.

So please don't think of this process as an ass-whoopin. Neither one of us have ever made any progress that way, and wouldn't impose that on anyone else. If anything, we are the anti-whoopin' patrol. Accountability work is far deeper than that, which is difficult, but also it is far more compassionate which makes it sustainable.

So let's start off with your current self-hatred messages and reframe them with compassionate accountability. It's ok if it doesn't feel authentic yet. We're gonna believe you aren't a piece of shit until you agree with us. On a piece of paper, make two columns. Label one "self-hatred" and one "compassionate accountability." And for each one reframe the negative messages playing on repeat in your head. The first column might say "I'm just a toxic and useless person," and the second column could be "I'm working to become more conscious of my patterns so I can better live up to my expectations for myself." With time and conscious thought, you will begin to erode years of shame and understand the person that you want to be.

Self-Hatred	Compassionate Accountability
I'm a toxic and useless person	I'm working to become more conscious of my patterns so I can better live up to my expectations for myself

How Can You Reframe Your Experience?

One of the places in which we get stuck is when we frame the story through the lens of how we were the victims of the violence or neglect of others. While those feelings are valid, they impede recovery. Rewriting our story as one in which we survived can dramatically reframe our experience without letting anyone off the hook for the harm they have caused. Once we realize our capacity to survive, we can then focus on our future goals instead of being stuck in the past. Try re-narrating your experience, placing yourself as the survivor instead of the victim:

S.O.L.V.E. Your Problem

This tool (adapted from *Dr. Weisinger's Anger Workout Book*) is an even more structured way of mapping out and creating solutions. It helps get your thinking brain back online when your emotional (angry) brain is trying to take over the show.

State Your Problem: Identify and define the problematic situation.

Outline Your Response: After describing the details of your problem as specifically and expansively as you can, then detail your usual response. Researchers who studied expert problem solvers found that they didn't look at the problems in abstract terms, but instead focused very concretely on the "who, what, where, when, why, and how" facts.

List Your Alternatives: Brainstorm all your possible solutions. Yes, even "magical thinking" type solutions or "go back to bed and let it figure itself out" solutions. They bubble up, and that's ok. Don't worry about quality, the important thing is quantity. Come up with as many different possibilities as possible.

Visualize Your Consequences: Consider the possible outcomes of all of the alternatives you listed. What might happen in both the short and long term? Are these consequences you can deal with? Cross out anything that is clearly a non-starter. Consider combining alternatives and visualizing how that would work.

Evaluate Your Results: Now you gotta act. Use the same strategy in more than one scenario (you know, on multiple occasions when people piss you off). What are the actual consequences? Is this an improvement over the old ways you responded? Do you need to go back to the drawing board, or do you have a good handle on things now?

Figuring Out Our Stuck Points

One of the biggest obstacles to forgiveness is our human tendency to keep reacting to hurt in the same ways, despite the fact that these strategies don't serve us. "Well, stop it" is an easy enough response, but human brains do so adore well-worn grooves of behavior…and we have to recognize the grooves before we can apply the brakes. This worksheet is designed to help you figure out your strategy for getting past stuck points by building conscious awareness of your behavior patterns so you can implement a plan for different ways of reacting.

New Strategy Experiment	Outcome of Experiment	Emotional Response

Old Strategy	Old Result	Emotional Response

Gratitude Journaling

There is a huge amount of research around gratitude and how helpful it is for our mental well-being. Gratitude helps us build more positive relationships, reduces depression, increases resilience, improves our physical health, increases empathy, decreases depression, and improves quality and quantity of sleep, to name just a few research findings.

How so? Gratitude journaling activates two different parts of the brain, the hypothalamus (stress regulator) and the ventral tegmental area (the reward system activator). So at the same time we are reducing stress, we are creating the sensation of winning a (little, tiny) lottery by increasing serotonin and dopamine—which is why some gratitude researchers call gratitude a "natural antidepressant."

Gratitude journaling seems to work best when you don't do it exactly the same way every day—it's good to build a habit, but if it becomes too much of a habit, the benefits decrease over time. So we've provided a bunch of prompts below. You can fill out a different one every day or a couple times a week, or copy them into a journal you are going to use in the longer term.

Small, daily comforts I am grateful for

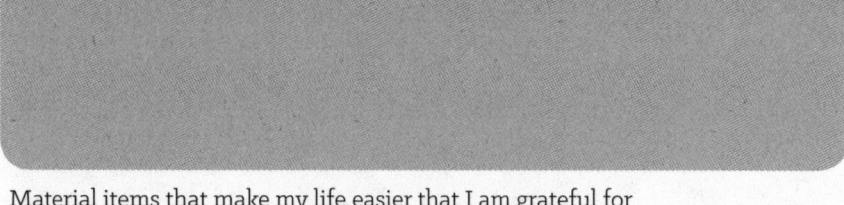

Material items that make my life easier that I am grateful for

Beauty in the world that I am grateful for

Kindness of others that I am grateful for

My healthy stress management skills that I am grateful for

New skills I have learned that I am grateful for

Tasks I have accomplished that I am grateful for

Future plans I have created that I am grateful for

Ways I have demonstrated compassion that I am grateful for

Self-care strategies I have used that I am grateful for

Positive thinking changes that I am grateful for

Healthy boundaries I have developed that I am grateful for

Intention Setting

Most of us are used to the idea of goal setting. Goals are about specific, measurable, and quantifiable outcomes. And goal setting is important, so we are not suggesting to give that up, in fact, we have a lot of exercises focused on those coming up. But...in day to day life there are many things that are out of our control that can affect our goal attainment (COVID-19 in 2020, anyone?).

Intention setting is about how we focus our energy on a day to day basis. It's about what we set our minds to notice. If you are looking to purchase a new bike, you are going to notice the bikes around you in a completely different way, right?

Intentions are about how we want to interact in the world, what we want to notice, and who we want to be. This will end up supporting our goal attainment.

You can consciously pay attention to opportunities to advance your goals but successful humaning stands apart (and above) our goal achievement. So let's start with our locus of control.

Things I do not have control over

Things I have control over

In some way shape or form, your answers centered on the fact that you do not have control over the behaviors of others, but you do have control over yourself right? This is important for intention setting, because whatever you set needs to be grounded in your own locus of control. While "I don't want to argue with anyone" is a nice goal to have, you don't have control over their argumentative nature of someone else. An intention of "I will presume the best intent of those around me" will go a long way to prevent you from starting an argument and will go a long way in helping you manage an argument that you get invited to participate in by someone else, right?

A week of intentionally

My intention for the week:

	Sunday	Monday	Tuesday	Wednesday	Thursday	Friday	Saturday
Progress							
Struggles							
What I noticed							

My overall wins: In which ways was I successful with my intention?

My overall growth opportunities: Where did I most struggle?

Is this an intention that is of benefit to me? Do I want to carry it forward or make any adjustments?

Accountability WOOP

I know, we've all heard a lot about visualizing the outcome you want. But Psychology professor Gabriele Oettingen found that fantasizing about making something happen has—surprisingly—a negative effect on our ability to make it happen. She noticed after coming to the U.S. from Germany that we have a cultural norm of "we can do anything!" while her upbringing was more pragmatic. Not necessarily negative, but German culture is more grounded in reality and thoughtful about goal setting. So she studied how Americans interacted with their goals differently and how this played out.

The brain tells stories to retain information and plan for safety. The brain does this with so much realism that it tricks us into thinking the story is the reality. So a fantasy about changing a behavior feels like we actually already changed the behavior, rather than a mental rehearsal planning session. So we become less likely to do the actual behavioral change work.

If we are mindful that fantasizing is only the first step in goal acquisition and use it to propel us to the next step, we can overcome that irritating brain quirk and increase our likelihood of achieving our goals. Dr. Oettingen came up with the Wish, Outcome, Obstacle, Plan (WOOP) framework to help us. Dr. Oettingen and her team created an app for WOOPing if you want to digitize your badassery. Or you can use this worksheet:

Wish—What is it that you are wanting to accomplish, achieve, or change? It's okay for it to be a reach, but it should be a feasible reach. Essentially, what's the goal?

Outcome—How will achieving this goal make you feel? What's your best result? Really lean into why this achievement could be important for you.

Obstacle—What is the main obstacle inside you that may get in the way of your achievement. This ties back to intention setting in that it's about what you have control over, not how you are hoping other people respond. If we were using asking someone out as an example, the obstacle might be your shyness in asking them, not that they might say no.

Plan—What is an effective way of managing that obstacle. Make a "when/then" plan. An example would be "when I feel overwhelmed by everything there is to do, then I will set the time and work for ten minutes on the project then take a break."

Accountability Goal Setting

You've done a ton of hard work so far in this workbook, getting better acquainted with your internal experiences and working with new tools that we designed to help you work toward being your better self. . Now you have the foundation to do the real heavy lifting of your accountability work. That's what you came here for, right? Let's get to it.

1) What, exactly, do you want to change about yourself? State this in positive and behaviorally focused terms, e.g. "I want to listen to the viewpoints of others without interrupting in order to understand where they are coming from" is far more doable than "I want to stop being a judgemental asshole."

2) Why do you want to change this about yourself? Why is this a personal priority?

3) How will making these changes improve your life?

4) How do you hope these changes will improve life for people you care about?

5) How do you hope these changes will impact future relationships?

6) Will anyone in your life be negatively affected by this change? Remember that any change to a system affects the whole system. Even good change can throw others into disequilibrium. If you stop drinking, others can no longer play the role of rescuing and enabling, for example. Those roles may be their way of not having to work through their own shit and they may have a negative reaction to you.

7) What do you think would be a reasonable timeline to actualize this change?

8) How much time will you need to set aside each week to work on making this happen? For what specific activities? How will they fit into your schedule?

9) What are some harmful or painful memories or experiences from your past that you haven't yet fully resolved?

10) What feedback and criticisms have other people given to you or have you heard second hand about your behavior? Why do you think people say them?

11) Which of these criticisms can you accept as valid and apply to your own behavior?

12) Which of these pieces of feedback about your behavior do you feel like don't apply and are probably other people's stuff?

13) What help do you need in making this change happen? Who can you rely upon for that help who would understand where you are coming from?

14) Where can you research best practices from people who have overcome this problem in the past? Can you reach out to them directly?

15) What are your best practices for moving forward? What are the actionable steps?

16) Make a list of your values:

17) What are some actionable steps to live closer to your values?

18) What are three incidents when your intent was good but your impact was damaging?

19) When you aren't too bummed out, make a list of the things that you've lost as a result of the behavior that you want to change. If you are working with a therapist, coach, sponsor, etc., getting support for this part may be of benefit to you.

20) Make a list of your needs:

21) How do you attempt to fulfill your needs and/or medicate your pain now?

22) What are some other possible strategies to get these needs met that you are willing to experiment with trying?

23) What is your motivation in acting out your current behaviors? What caused them in the first place?

24) Who can help keep you accountable to these changes you want to make?

25) What circumstances and relationships in your life now are holding you back from your goal? Who is helping you achieve it?

26) Are you finding yourself falling into patterns of feeling shame and judging yourself? How so?

27) What are some ways you can challenge those thoughts, feelings, and reactions?

28) Where and with whom are you succeeding?

29) Where and with whom are you struggling?

30) Who is one person you can apologize to without causing further damage to them? What are you apologizing for?

31) What are some ways that you can make amends for how you've hurt this person and betrayed their trust?

32) How can you demonstrate long term change as you progress?

33) How will you know when you've succeeded and have been accountable?

34) What are some ways that you can give back to help other people who have struggled in the same areas and ways as yourself?

PROGRESS LOG, WEEK ONE:

Rate Your Success ☆ ☆ ☆ ☆ ☆

What are three things that you're thankful about?

_____

_____

_____

Who in your life now is holding you back from your goal? Who is helping you achieve it?

_____

_____

Are you finding yourself falling into patterns of feeling shame and judging yourself?

_____

Where are you succeeding?

_____

_____

Where are you struggling?

_____

_____

Who is one person that you can apologize to? Why?

_____

How could you make amends with how you've hurt this person and betrayed their trust?

_____

How can you demonstrate longterm change as you progress?

_____

_____

_____

PROGRESS LOG, WEEK TWO: Rate Your Success ☆ ☆ ☆ ☆ ☆

What are three things that you're thankful about?

___

___

___

Who in your life now is holding you back from your goal? Who is helping you achieve it?

___

___

Are you finding yourself falling into patterns of feeling shame and judging yourself?

___

Where are you succeeding?

___

___

Where are you struggling?

___

___

Who is one person that you can apologize to? Why?

___

How could you make amends with how you've hurt this person and betrayed their trust?

___

How can you demonstrate longterm change as you progress?

___

___

___

Review, repeat, and challenge yourself every day.

PROGRESS LOG, WEEK THREE:
Rate Your Success ☆ ☆ ☆ ☆ ☆

What are three things that you're thankful about?

_____
_____
_____

Who in your life now is holding you back from your goal? Who is helping you achieve it?

_____
_____

Are you finding yourself falling into patterns of feeling shame and judging yourself?

_____

Where are you succeeding?

_____
_____

Where are you struggling?

_____
_____

Who is one person that you can apologize to? Why?

_____

How could you make amends with how you've hurt this person and betrayed their trust?

_____

How can you demonstrate longterm change as you progress?

_____
_____
_____

Review, repeat, and challenge yourself every day.

PROGRESS LOG, WEEK FOUR:
Rate Your Success ☆ ☆ ☆ ☆ ☆

What are three things that you're thankful about?

_____

_____

_____

Who in your life now is holding you back from your goal? Who is helping you achieve it?

_____

_____

Are you finding yourself falling into patterns of feeling shame and judging yourself?

_____

Where are you succeeding?

_____

_____

Where are you struggling?

_____

_____

Who is one person that you can apologize to? Why?

_____

How could you make amends with how you've hurt this person and betrayed their trust?

_____

How can you demonstrate longterm change as you progress?

_____

_____

_____

Review, repeat, and challenge yourself every day.

PROGRESS LOG, WEEK FIVE:

Rate Your Success ☆ ☆ ☆ ☆ ☆

What are three things that you're thankful about?

___

___

Who in your life now is holding you back from your goal? Who is helping you achieve it?

___

Are you finding yourself falling into patterns of feeling shame and judging yourself?

___

Where are you succeeding?

___

Where are you struggling?

___

Who is one person that you can apologize to? Why?

___

How could you make amends with how you've hurt this person and betrayed their trust?

___

How can you demonstrate longterm change as you progress?

___

___

___

Review, repeat, and challenge yourself every day.

PROGRESS LOG, WEEK SIX: Rate Your Success ☆ ☆ ☆ ☆ ☆

What are three things that you're thankful about?

___

___

___

Who in your life now is holding you back from your goal? Who is helping you achieve it?

___

___

Are you finding yourself falling into patterns of feeling shame and judging yourself?

___

Where are you succeeding?

___

___

Where are you struggling?

___

___

Who is one person that you can apologize to? Why?

___

How could you make amends with how you've hurt this person and betrayed their trust?

___

How can you demonstrate longterm change as you progress?

___

___

___

Review, repeat, and challenge yourself every day.

PROGRESS LOG, WEEK SEVEN: Rate Your Success ☆ ☆ ☆ ☆ ☆

What are three things that you're thankful about?

_____

_____

Who in your life now is holding you back from your goal? Who is helping you achieve it?

_____

_____

Are you finding yourself falling into patterns of feeling shame and judging yourself?

_____

Where are you succeeding?

_____

_____

Where are you struggling?

_____

_____

Who is one person that you can apologize to? Why?

_____

How could you make amends with how you've hurt this person and betrayed their trust?

_____

How can you demonstrate longterm change as you progress?

_____

_____

_____

Review, repeat, and challenge yourself every day.

PROGRESS LOG, WEEK EIGHT: Rate Your Success ☆ ☆ ☆ ☆ ☆

What are three things that you're thankful about?

_____

_____

_____

Who in your life now is holding you back from your goal? Who is helping you achieve it?

_____

_____

Are you finding yourself falling into patterns of feeling shame and judging yourself?

_____

Where are you succeeding?

_____

_____

Where are you struggling?

_____

_____

Who is one person that you can apologize to? Why?

_____

How could you make amends with how you've hurt this person and betrayed their trust?

_____

How can you demonstrate longterm change as you progress?

_____

_____

_____

Review, repeat, and challenge yourself every day.

PROGRESS LOG, WEEK NINE: Rate Your Success ☆ ☆ ☆ ☆ ☆

What are three things that you're thankful about?

_____
_____
_____

Who in your life now is holding you back from your goal? Who is helping you achieve it?

_____
_____

Are you finding yourself falling into patterns of feeling shame and judging yourself?

_____

Where are you succeeding?

_____
_____

Where are you struggling?

_____
_____

Who is one person that you can apologize to? Why?

_____

How could you make amends with how you've hurt this person and betrayed their trust?

_____

How can you demonstrate longterm change as you progress?

_____
_____
_____

Review, repeat, and challenge yourself every day.

Achieve Your Goals

In-depth goal setting is essential to change your behavior. You need to know where and how you want to be. No matter what you're working on—saving up, getting a new job, ending a cycle of violence, respecting your family, or a relationship change—you probably have some sense by now of what is the biggest thing you want to work on to get you aligned with your values and dreams.

Getting our goals down into a workable format is what makes them achievable. Breaking your ideal self into traits shows your own progress.

What, exactly, is your goal? What do you desire? State this in positive terms. Not what you don't want but what you really, really want. Choose something that is in your control. Not "I want my partner to stop drinking." You can only control yourself, after all, right?

Now describe your goal in sensory-specific terms. What will you see, hear, and feel when you achieve this goal?

Is this goal achievable? Is this something you can get done? You know, REASONABLY.

So presuming we passed the achievable test, now ask yourself if it is realistic? That is, is it worth your time and commitment. Take some time to jot down notes on the following questions. What sacrifices do I have to make in pursuit of this goal? How will this affect my life in both negative and positive ways? And while you're at it, whose goal is this really? Is it a goal that a parent or partner has encouraged you toward but it isn't really what you want for YOURSELF? If you pursue that goal, then, does it mean that you real goal is to please someone in your life by earning this achievement instead of earning the achievement itself?

Does this goal align with your value system? Think about your moral compass for a moment. Whether it be spiritual or secular. Is what you are wanting to accomplish in alignment with what you consider to be important about who you are and how you interact with the world around you?

What is the timeline for this goal? What's a reasonable amount of time to spend on this? What amount of time are you willing to spend on this?

How will the work you need to put into achieving this goal affect the people around you? What impact will it have on the people who are important in your life. List both positive and negative impacts.

You made a list of things you may lose or give up in the process. Are there any ways of mitigating those losses?

What else will achieving this goal do for you? What are your side gains? If your goal is to go back to school, what will doing so give you other than a new degree or certification?

How will you know when you've achieved this goal? If your goal is moving to a new city, that's easy. When you are in the new city, you've achieved your goal. But answering this question can be way harder than it looks, right? When people tell me, for example, that their goal is to be happy and I ask them to explain what happy looks like, I usually get feedback like "I want to have a positive relationship with my partner and enjoy my career. To me, those are goals are more about being connected and fulfilled than happy. When you start looking at your markers of achievement, you may realize that your goal wording needs to shift somewhat. Good deal. Go ahead and shift away.

Why have you not achieved this goal already? What has gotten in your way in the past?

What obstacles are still in your path in the present? What obstacles may come up in the future?

Which of these obstacles do you have control over? What is your plan for managing them?

Which obstacles are out of your control? What resources can you use to work around them?

Who can help you or be an accountability partner for you?

What have you done already that is moving you in the direction of achieving this goal?

What would be the next step?

What is your action plan and time line for taking the next step?

After completing this step, what did you learn? Is there anything you need to shift after this point of action?

Based on what you completed already, and what you learned in the process, what's the next step? (This is the place where you lather, rinse, repeat through goal completion.)

90-Day Skill Challenge

In the next 90 days, I want to improve at:

Every day you practice the skill, mark off the day, or use a sticker, or color it in.

HOW YOU RELATE TO OTHERS

Frightened Selves

- approach conversations to change minds
- express yourself to look cool and signify membership of a group 
- use language to assert authority and dominance 
- exclude people because of how their character has been portrayed 
- portray a false image on social media 
- get lost in theory 
- weaponize identity 
- don't understand people with backgrounds and experiences unlike their own 
- believe utopia is an impossibility so change isn't worth the effort 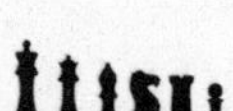

Authentic Selves

- listen to others without an agenda
- express themselves authentically, being open to others 
- simplify complicated concepts 
- help others recognize mistakes and missteps and how to do better 
- help others to relate to shared lived experiences 
- committed to action in pursuit of values 
- recognizing others identity and struggles to create closeness 
- build solidarity amongst a variety of people with different experiences 
- build the world they want to see from the ground up! 

© Joe Biel, 2021, JoeBiel.net, This poster and other infographics like it are available from www.Microcosm.Pub

Change Your Relationships

As brain science continues to tell us, we are a species that is hardwired for relationships. We need relationships to survive. But it doesn't mean we always do a good job at maintaining them, which is why we need to learn the skill of accountability in our relationships, personal lives, and professional lives. Some conflict is inevitable simply as a result of wound up feelings, stress, bad days, and unresolved simmering tensions. It's how we acknowledge, address, and resolve these things that makes all of the difference.

Your best and primary method for handling conflict is handling your own reactions but, failing that, you will need other strategies when conflict still inevitably arises. Throughout this book—and much moreso in the accompanying handbook—we have included various frameworks and guides for understanding and handling conflict. The type of skill to employ will depend on the type of relationship. You have different types of relationships with your partner, your friend, your mail carrier, your grocery clerk, your coworkers, etc. Different relationships have various intensities and problems so we created a pretty wide set of tools.

Different proximities of relationships and different desired outcomes require different types of solutions. There are power dynamics and differentials everywhere and you must be mindful of them—especially when conflict rears up. Because ultimately, the person with the most power also has the most responsibility to patch things up. So if that is you, it's doubly important to listen. And while many have tried, you can't resolve most disputes through subordination. It's winning the battle to lose the war. Really the only time that holding power over someone is an appropriate strategy is when you are dealing with your child, a pet who can't take care of itself, someone who is incapable of making their own choices at this time, or someone that you manage at work—cases where the stated relationship is subordinate, so doing so is likely not manipulation. Conflict mediator Lauren Gross explains "conflicts can actually be a good way to build a relationship. If needs are met, you both feel heard and you can meet each other where you are at, relationships can actually become stronger through conflict. When the other person digs in their heels, it means that they are committed to their position and often the need to be right. What is that underlying need though? It's really important to figure that out. Once you do, there is a lot more room to be creative in how to meet that need and them to meet yours."

It's important to think of relationships not as a binary but as a spectrum. You will have different kinds of relationships and conflicts with different kinds of people. There are things that you would tell your partner but not your mail man or your boss. Sometimes it can feel easier to confide in a stranger, because there is no risk of abandonment and the consequences are fewer. Similarly, there are things that you can really only trust with your closest friends with whom you have invested the most emotional intimacy and time. This is partially because they understand where you are coming from but also because they have opted into this situation. The people that we are closest to are the ones where we risk the most painful conflict because we are so invested. This is, again, because we feel that we should be on the same page about all things so it's painful when we can't understand each other. Your values are the most important thing to consider when you allow new people into your closest sphere of relationships. Conversely, not consciously choosing whom you trust and allow to be close to you is also a choice, albeit one not likely to be in your best interest.

While it would be nice to have a magic wand we could wave and change other people's behavior, we cannot. But you know what we can do? Change our own behavior, how we respond to others' behavior, and create boundaries that ultimately protect us. Here are some tools to help you with that.

Relationships Inventory

Let's assess all your current relationships. Family, friends, partners, lovers, coworkers, neighbors, acquaintances—anyone currently in your life. Start by listing them and what kind of relationship you have with them:

Name	Type of Relationship	Closeness 1-10	Should this change?

Circle of Closeness

Now write in the names of people in your life into these concentric circles, depending on how close you feel to them:

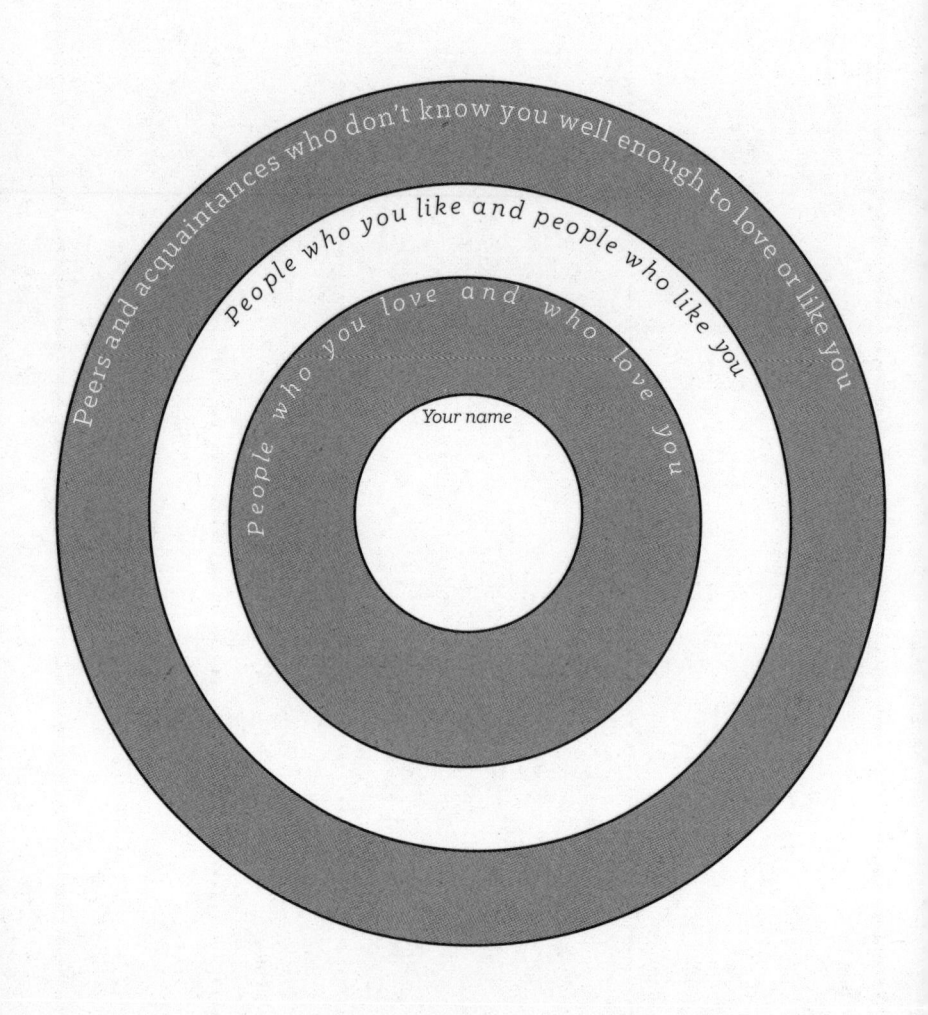

- Peers and acquaintances who don't know you well enough to love or like you
- People who you like and people who like you
- People who you love and who love you
- Your name

I Statements

If we taught "I statement" communication in kindergarten, Faith wouldn't have a job. It invokes a language of responsibility for our own emotional content, while sharing with others how their behavior has informed our emotional content.

Communicating in this way is going to feel weird and difficult at first, because it simply isn't how people discuss their emotions in this country.

Faith's favorite story is the client she had years ago who started her I statement by saying *"I feel you're being an asshole!"* Funny as hell. Not an I statement.

Some better examples:

I feel anxious when your voice gets loud during discussions. What I want is for you to not raise your voice to me.

Extra credit for explaining the "why" of what you're feeling, like this:

I feel frustrated and hurt when you agree to do the dishes before I get home and you don't do them. What I want is for you to follow through on tasks you agreed to complete. I feel cared for when you prioritize something that is important to me and I like coming home to a clean kitchen so I can start dinner right away because I'm generally starving by then.

You can even take an extra step in acknowledging that they didn't intend the distress you felt. This can go a long way into disarming a potential fight. For instance:

I felt uncomfortable when you made that joke just now. I know you just meant it to be funny and thought I would laugh rather than be upset. But I struggle with jokes about that topic because I was bullied a lot in school about that. I would really appreciate it if you didn't tell jokes like that around me.

Try this with your partner when you are all kinds of hacked off (or all kinds of thrilled, for that matter). Here's a good chance to practice using some of the more common issues that come up for you and the people you have to communicate with on a regular basis.

I feel _____

when you _____

What I want is _____

I feel _____

when you _____

What I want is _____

I feel _____

when you _____

What I want is _____

I feel _____

when you _____

What I want is _____

I feel _____

when you _____

What I want is _____

I feel _____

when you _____

What I want is _____

I feel _____

when you _____

What I want is _____

I feel _____

when you _____

What I want is _____

The Four Levels of Communication

We are all trying to communicate mo' better. Communicating with "I statements" model is a great strategy for being more mindful of that process. But figuring out where the breakdowns come from the most often is also hugely beneficial.

The basic idea is that each exchange of verbal dialogue has four levels:

1. **What we mean to say.** You know, the actual idea you are trying to express.

2. **What we actually say.** If you are really good at only saying exactly what you mean at all times, you are a rock star and we hope you write a book on your technique. For us regular humans, what we have in our minds and what comes out of our mouths is not always a solid match.

3. **What the other person hears.** Just because you said it doesn't mean they heard it without any filter.

4. **What the other person thinks you mean.** Even if you said "anything for dinner is fine" and you meant anything for dinner is fine, your partner may think there is a hidden agenda, or other things going on beyond the words that actually came out of your mouth.

Every couple Faith has worked with who is struggling with a communication breakdown has a problem in at least one of these areas. Generally we are high achievers and are activating more than one if not all of them. Figuring out where the breakdown is occurring informs the strategies to repair it.

What levels of communication do you most often get stuck in?

What strategies can you try to prevent getting stuck?

What strategies can you try to repair when communication breaks down?

Apologies, Atonement, Forgiveness, and Repentance: Accountability in Action

Forgiveness is a universal human need. It is a topic for consideration in all religious texts and many philosophical ones (Kant most notably). It's one of the eight positive emotions, according to George Valliant. (And guess what? Compassion is another of the eight).

Forgiveness often sets the stage for relationship repair. While Faith has written quite a bit on forgiving others, here we are writing about putting accountability into action through the practice of requesting forgiveness. Forgiveness is only part of the repair process, however. In order to look at this work holistically, we ended up borrowing heavily from a 4000 years-old tradition.

Scholars of Judaism note significant differences between the terms "atonement," "forgiveness," and "repentance," which are incredibly helpful to our discussion here, if only as a philosophical stance. Meaning, you don't have to celebrate passover or worship any deities to find this helpful to your own internal work.

Repentance in Hebrew is "Tshuva" which means to return. So when we discuss our value system and moral alignment, think of repentance as a return to alignment. It minimizes our risk of causing more harm in the future, therefore is considered the work of ethical self-transformation. We can always grow and change and become better even though we can't often undo past harm. We can take responsibility, repair as much as possible, and do better in the future.

If repentance is our internal work, our outward expression of that work takes place within forgiveness and atonement. Forgiveness is the hoped-for outcome of our expression of regret through apology, and atonement is the actions we take beyond our apology to create healing. Repentance work, then, is a lengthy process, not just a tearful voicemail (or press conference, as the case may be).

Rabbi Danya Ruttenberg explains the steps to repentance work as follows. For each one, explain how you could achieve it and how it fits your specific situation.

Owning the harm perpetrated (ideally, publicly to your community)

Doing the work to become the kind of person who doesn't do harm (which requires a ton of inner work)

Making restitution for harm done, in whatever way possible

Then apologizing for the harm caused in whatever way that will make it as right as possible with the victim

When faced with the opportunity to cause similar harm in the future, make a better choice.

The Three R's of An Apology

A true apology is as rare as unpolluted urban air. We're not sure if it's always been the case in human history, but damn, humans suck at apologizing.

The three most popular apology formats are also deeply shitty:

- The dismiss and move forward ("Stop being upset, you're too sensitive, it was funny!")
- The political no-responsibility apology ("I'm sorry if people were upset")
- The half-assed sorry/not sorry apology. ("I'm sorry I upset you, it was just a joke!")

As a therapist, Faith presumes that apologizing is difficult because true accountability requires a level of vulnerability with which we are deeply uncomfortable, so anyone doing the difficult work of authentic apologizing has our deepest respect. Her model of an authentic apology is a 3-Rs model, meaning **Responsibility**, **recognition**, and **repair**. Let us explain what we mean by these terms.

Responsibility is the easy one. It refers to ownership of the harm caused without explanation or equivocation. No "buts," not "I didn't mean it" (I'm gonna presume you didn't mean it, at least the vast majority of the time). Just "I see that my words/actions (or lack thereof) caused pain. Because they were my words/actions (or lack thereof), I am responsible for that pain and I am sorry that I caused it."

The second part is **recognition**. This is where we open ourselves to a deeper understanding of the harm we caused. Of course, we cannot force someone to hear or accept an apology from us, and we definitely cannot force them to revisit the issue in detail but we can invite them into a dialogue in which we learn more, and grow more as humans. It means asking for a deeper understanding of how something we said/did (or didn't say/do) caused harm, and then shutting-up and committing to listening without intention of response. Recognition helps us be better people because it gives us the context surrounding our harm, allowing us to better generalize the lesson to other aspects of our lives. Recognition asks "If you are willing to share more about how my actions hurt you, I would like to hear you. I am committed to working on myself as a human being, which means more listening and understanding."

And why? Why would we go that extra step? Because according to relational-cultural theory, that's where the real relationship work happens. Disconnection is an unavoidable part of relationships. Disconnection can lead to further alienation or it can be our opportunity to do the vulnerable work of **repair**. Where a facetious or dismissive apology creates anger and shame, repair creates authenticity, empathy, and growth. Repair isn't only atonement. Acknowledging that you hear and confirm how your actions have affected someone else is repair. Showing someone that you believe their experience is real can help make them whole again.

Now write your own apology utilizing the three Rs. It's better to keep it short, lest you ramble into dangerous territory or making excuses. So give it some good thought and re-read the above before you start writing. We have plenty of examples of good and bad apologies in the accompanying handbook.

Gaslighting-Proof Yourself

Gaslighting is the term for when someone habitually tries to convince you that what you see and remember is false. For example, you might clearly remember them hitting you or insulting you, but they lie about it and claim that you're delusional, crazy, or misinterpreting the situation. After a while, it's easy to start distrusting your own perceptions, even in other situations and with other people. Maybe you were gaslit as a kid, or by a partner or employer. Or maybe you've used gaslighting to try to gain power over other people or in situations.

In situations when you are being gaslit, here are some sample responses that hold your ground without escalating conflict:

- "We remember things differently."
- "If you to speak to me this way, I'm ending the discussion."
- "I hear you and that's not my experience."
- "I'm taking some time away from this conversation."
- "I know my truth and we don't need to discuss it."

If you aren't sure about how you feel about something, spend a few minutes being aware of your thoughts, feelings, and body sensations. Write them down. You'll see how your body knows how you feel better than your thinking brain does. Write about what you realized, what you learned, and what it means for the future.

STAGNATING LEADERS | EFFECTIVE LEADERS

STAGNATING LEADERS	EFFECTIVE LEADERS
Power comes from authority	Power comes from collaboration
Privatizes information	Shares information
Discourages team from developing ideas	Encourages suggestions and ideas
Dictates solutions to problems	Collectivizes solutions to problems
Minimizes time & resources for problem solving	Allocates time and resources to prevent problems
Believes in strict roles & responsibilities	Roles and responsibilities are fluid and evolve
Deals reactively to problems	Resolves root causes of problems
Reviews staff performance once per year	Provides immediate and ongoing feedback and personalized coaching

© Joe Biel, 2019, JoeBiel.net, This poster and other infographics like it are available from www.Microcosm.Pub

Problem Solving with Others

As we've made clear throughout this book, you can only be accountable to yourself. But what about when you've legitimately been wronged? Is there anything that you can do?

Conflict is as unpredictable as it is inevitable. You will be scooting along, having a wonderful day, when someone else identifies conflict with you. Or worse, they will be scooting along and you'll identify conflict with them. With the tools to deal with it, it's fine. Life is like that. And it's better to deal with the conflict than to ignore or avoid it.

A common example of dealing with conflict is cheating on a partner. As a couples therapist, Faith treats infidelity as a form of interpersonal trauma for the partner who was cheated on. (All good therapists steal from other therapists and this approach to working with infidelity was influenced by the trauma-informed work of Barry McCarthy who was in turn influenced by Snyder, Baucom, and Gordon.) Faith is first and foremost a trauma therapist, and this approach makes intuitive sense to her. But Faith takes this a step further and presumes the event was also traumatic to the partner who cheated.

Sure, some people are merely acting selfishly with no regard for the feelings of others and no remorse for their behavior. If that's the case in your relationship, the hard truth is that the cheated-on person doesn't have a relationship with the cheater based on respect for them and their needs. You've been handed an ultimatum and you need to decide whether or not it's one you can live with. For everyone else? Yes, the person who was cheated on is clearly, unequivocally injured by what happened. And so is the person who cheated. They did something that was out of alignment to commitments they made and probably (hopefully) to their personal ethical code. It's a form of moral injury that requires attention and work.

Overall—no matter your conflict—your best strategy is to be altruistic 96% of the time. Presume best intent. It's you two against the problem, not against each other. Altruism, the selfless concern for others' wellbeing, comes from evolutionary motivations to maintain a cohesive group that can protect itself. Melanie Billings-Yun's Beyond Dealmaking suggests that negotiation only works when the outcome remains in everyone's best interest and that the best way forward is "tit-for-tat." If the other party is uncooperative, so are you. If the other party rewards, you reward them as well. It sounds savage but it's essentially setting a boundary that you expect altruism. Mirroring the behavior of the other party is almost always the most beneficial act for everyone. Doing so builds trust and approval. Kindness is rewarded with kindness and standing within the group will improve as a result of it. And frankly, being altruistic is just less exhausting than being constantly distrustful of everything and everyone's motives.

Sometimes ongoing conflict is a source for greater personal reflection. As Joe came to realize later in life, you shouldn't remain friends with someone just because they are available and willing. Joe now knows not to keep friends who don't take Joe's autism seriously and who endeavor to understand it; just like how someone who uses a wheelchair for mobility shouldn't hang out with anyone who demands they just get up and walk. Additionally, after age 40, Joe focused on friendships with individuals who were relatively similar in age and/or life experiences, otherwise the power differential was lopsided and possibly harmful to the younger individual. And honestly, it results in far less conflict and much more relating.

Our brains respond to new situations in an old way for all of the reasons that we've outlined in the previous chapters: usually because a conflict has triggered a previous trauma. Sometimes just being activated feels like being triggered and our brain moves into high alert: Flight! Fight! Freeze! We have to practice our CBT skills to get back to our thinking brain.

Instead, when you find yourself getting angry, start by telling yourself the whole story about what happened. Humanize the situation by asking yourself to list all of the various reasons why a reasonable, rational person would behave the way that the person that you have conflict with did. Employ genuine curiosity. If you're having trouble calming your panic and accessing your thinking brain, do what Navy Seals do: breathe in for four seconds then breathe out for four seconds.

Ask yourself: are you being bullied or are you being disagreed with? Intellectually, we all know someone doesn't have to agree with us, but in the moment, disagreement can feel like being bullied. Is the other person trying to tell you what your experience should be? Are they speaking for themselves or for you? Are they stating their opinion or insisting that they know what's best for you?

The exception to the 96% rule is when the other party consistently has shown nefarious motives and has repeatedly demonstrated that you cannot trust them. Just from reading the previous sentence, you know if you have encountered a character like this. If someone has repeatedly shown that you can't trust them, what are you doing in the relationship? If someone is holding you hostage and refusing to do things as were agreed, such as threatening you with consequences or enacting systems of control, you need to address this. This kind of interaction makes everyone miserable and turns everything into a power struggle while you feel like a prisoner. In this last section, we've provided some tools to hold boundaries in one-on-one settings or in a group.

The Radical Adventure Riders, a bicycle touring and camping group, created a pledge to make the cycling industry more responsible for making workplaces, communities, and the world genuinely inclusive. We have found that these same principles are a solid starting point for problem solving with others, so we are sharing them here with permission (and with some revisions of our own). This is not about beating ourselves up or being so upset at our past behavior that we never leave the house again. It is about recognizing that when we know better, we can do better. Being embarrassed by our past behaviors is a good sign that means we are continuously growing. Accountability means doing the work we need to do in order to continuously grow. When we are able to process "in this situation, I really upset someone I care about because I presumed…" we are building the neural pathways that help us remember to not make that same mistake in the future.

1. Trust Intent, Acknowledge Impact

We have to trust each other to work together, but we may hurt each other along the way. Listen when you have harmed. Harm is about the effect of our actions, not our objective. When have you harmed someone? How did your impact differ from your intent? How did you harm the other party? What did you learn?

2. Practice Consent

Ask for consent before touching people or their stuff, when giving advice, and taking photos. Don't presume that consent is easy for someone to give you. Recognize that power differentials may make it more difficult for someone to express both "no" and "yes." Strive to recognize power-over dynamics, however unintentional, and work to shift them to power-with dynamics to whatever extent is possible.

When have you needed to step back and ask for consent outside of the bedroom?

3. Honor Language an Individual Chooses for Themselves

No policing of identities. No comparing your perceptions of someone's outsides to their understanding of their insides. When have you needed to show more respect for how others see themselves or their identities?

4. Don't Assume, Let People Share, or Ask When Appropriate

Do not make assumptions about gender, race, ability, skill level, or knowledge. When have you hurt someone by making assumptions?

5. Avoid Harmful Language

Pay attention to your habits of language. We all use words that are problematic without realising it, especially those of us who are older. Avoid ableist, ageist, racist and gendered language. When is a time that you unintentionally used language that excluded others? What did you learn?

6. Do Not Shame

We come here from a wide variety of experience levels, financial access, and opportunities. Shame is an attack on personhood, not a recognition of a mistake that someone has made. No call-outs. When is a time—intentional or not—that you shamed someone? How could you have made them feel included or supported?

7. Work Towards Collective Understanding

No body or mind can be left behind—only moving together can we accomplish what we require. When is a time that you could have included someone or a group but didn't?

8. Recognize Wholeness

People have inherent worth outside of productivity. As a result, we acknowledge the necessity for rest and self-love. When have you needed to remember to rest and love yourself instead of being productive?

9. Make Space and Step Back

Make intentional space for people of color, indigenous and trans people. How have you taken up too much space or centered your own experience at the expense of someone else?

Talking Out Conflict

If there's one definitive thing that we can say about conflict, it's that it's unpredictable and inconsistent. Here are some additional skills, further understanding, and coping strategies for handling various kinds of breakdowns during a conversation about conflict. Much of this applies to people that you are closer to, where emotional proximity is tantamount to the relationship, like a close friend, parent, or partner, but it can also apply to groups where feelings run hot.

It's deeply unfair to ascribe your own meaning to things when you don't really know what the other person is thinking or feeling. Would you like someone to make those assumptions about your thoughts and feelings? When we talk about accountability in the context of conflict, it's holding people accountable to prior agreements and group boundaries, not to your own value system.

When you find yourself holding malice or resentment, you need to talk about it. "I'd like to talk to you about what just happened," is a good icebreaker. If the other party isn't engaging in the conversation, there is a reason. When you are dominating the conversation on a subject of conflict, acknowledge any complaint the quieter party has. Ask why they aren't talking. Usually this means that they feel outgunned through guilt tripping, or being silenced, hounded, or dominated until they succumb. This may be because of how they were treated in previous relationships and conflict brings them back to that place. Acknowledging this creates safety. Give a chance for them to explain why it feels unsafe.

It's better to have these conversations in person or on the telephone so that people can react and information can freely move in both directions in real time. This exercise is adapted from Crucial Conversations: Tools for Talking When Stakes are High, one of the best books we found on accountability. Kerry Patterson, Joseph Grenny, Ron McMillan, and Al Switzler created a solution to help start a conversation, called Ask Mirror Paraphrase Prime (AMPP).

Ask: When there is conflict, what does the other person think is happening?

Mirror: Describe what you perceive to be their emotions. E.g. "You seem upset."

Paraphrase: Repeat what they say back to them in your own words to demonstrate comprehension. "It would be really frustrating to find out that we're going to see a movie when you believed we were going to the zoo."

Prime: Offer your best guess about how you believe that they perceive the larger issue and encourage them to speak more about the situation.

This is a good method to show that you are comfortable talking openly about the situation. Acknowledge that everyone wants to feel respected and included but doesn't always feel listened to. If the other person escalates, there is a good reason. Escalation is a distraction from the issue at hand because the person acting out doesn't have support or tools to address the underlying issue. If someone is angry, it's because they had a core value violated. In order to solve their issues, ask them to talk about them by retracing their path to action. E.g. "I have watched you prioritize other people for promotions ahead of me for years. If I didn't speak up now, you wouldn't even have considered me!" What was their path to action?

Often during an accountability conversation, another accountability issue will be brought up. Usually you'll want to focus on the most important conversation. Usually that's the prior topic that sparked the conversation. But sometimes new information will be revealed that will change what the most important conversation is. What new information came up during this conversation?

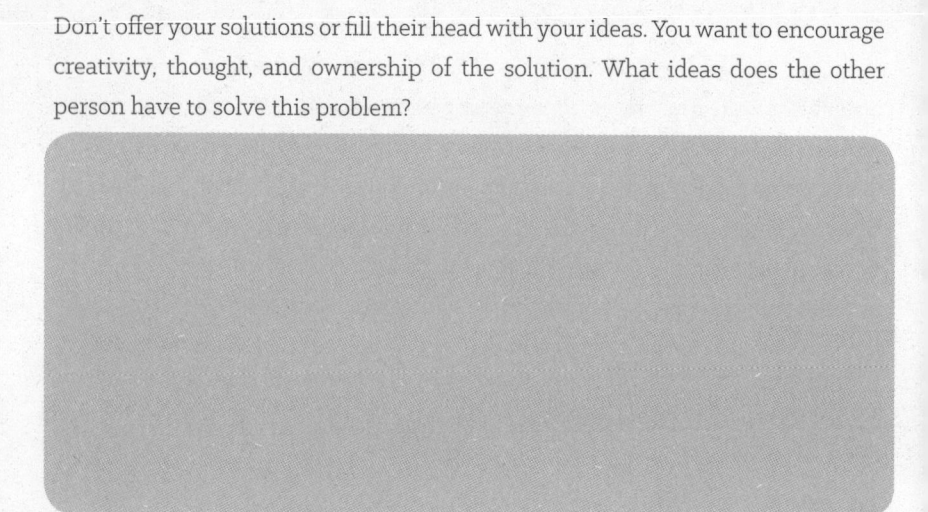

Don't offer your solutions or fill their head with your ideas. You want to encourage creativity, thought, and ownership of the solution. What ideas does the other person have to solve this problem?

Conflict in Groups

If there's a conflict but you aren't directly involved in it, things are a little different. A sample script to get started is "It's no secret that you and X aren't getting along. I was hoping that you might share your perspective and experiences so that we can try and resolve it. It's been going on too long and I think that resolution would be to everyone's benefit."

The key points here are that you aren't placing blame. You are looking at the facts and an objective language. You are respecting the experience of everyone involved, even if one person is creating the bulk of the problems. Avoid authoritarianism, focus on the rewards and benefits for each person and the group, and show how performing the desired behavior makes you part of the group.

What do the involved parties think would help? Try to assure them as best you can that healing the conflict is in the best interest of the organization. Use their brainstorm to help them feel invested in the outcome, and thus the group.

What are the maladaptive behaviors? Be as specific as possible.

What vague and unactionable accusations have been brought forward that you need to verify or eradicate?

What previous requests and boundaries have been ignored and by whom?

What is your specific schedule to get specific items done, with short, medium, and long term deadlines? Who will oversee each deadline?

Task	Date	Person Responsible

Who will advocate for each party that can double as a less emotional point of contact for information in both directions?

List each substantive step as an action plan to solving the problem

What are the if/then boundaries of the situation?

Action	Consequence

What better organizational boundaries do you think would prevent this, moving forward? If one person is consistently breaking rules and nobody has said anything, that's the organization's fault as much as the person's.

Therapy, Coaching, Mentoring, and Accountability Partnerships

While group accountability sessions haven't historically been helpful, the opinions of people that know us well enough to observe patterns can be. Especially if it is the people who don't have any kind of hidden negative agenda. Faith always says that if her best friend tells her she's being a bitch it's because...she's being a bitch. And he loves her and wants her to figure out why she's so cranky and adjust herself. He's not saying it to make her feel bad or silence her or whatever.

Joe has always been perplexed by the commonality of hearing one person admit to bad behavior and someone else commiserating in a way that lets them off the hook. Like, "Well of course you screamed at the barista, you were so frustrated and upset at that point, OMG!" Joe's autistic brain remains very confused that the commiserating friend wasn't saying, "That's such a hurtful and unproductive way to communicate. Is this how you interact with people when I'm not around? I'm really upset about this!" The research for this book led to the distinction between idiot compassion and wise compassion. Just like clean pain and dirty pain, compassion also exists in the dialectic. And it all made sense.

Idiot compassion is when you console someone for something that is really their own fault. Like if you said something insensitive or got fired from a job, it feels good to have a friend empathize. The problem is that it doesn't allow you to see your own role or encourage change. It serves to shift the blame and let you off the hook, rather than encourage reflection.

Wise compassion, on the other hand, is a friend loving you by asking questions about patterns in your behavior. While observations that hold truth can feel like an attack, when a friend that we trust exhibits wise compassion we are being offered a rare moment to reflect on the patterns in our life and how they are taking us away from who we want to be. And let's be honest. It's far easier to commiserate...so someone speaking to our patterns kindly is a gift that requires as much vulnerability on their part as it does on your part.

Wise compassion still starts with compassion. The idea that someone is hurting even if they hurt themselves or someone else. It's recognizing and validating their emotions as authentic even when the resulting behavior was hurtful.

> "I can tell that is a frustrating situation for you, but yelling at the barista is not who you are as a person. If you're overwhelmed right now, maybe I can help with that."
>
> "I'm so sorry you got fired from your job, I can tell you're angry and frustrated. You've really struggled to keep a job this year, I wonder if we can figure out the pattern and problem solve around it."

Faith refers to being this kind of friend (or therapist, or coach, or accountability partner) as being kind but not nice. Nice lets us off the hook and if we are off the hook we aren't doing the introspective work of change. Kind recognizes the struggle but still holds space for change. Kind tells someone "I know your heart and I want others to see it as well."

When you are experiencing hardship or difficult realizations, you can practice these skills with yourself. You can wallow in your own misery or you can look at your failure to suit everyone's needs using your thinking brain with a distanced objectivity. Remember, doing "bad things" does not make you a "bad person." You likely had a motivation with a different intent than the impact you had. So take some time to explore that as well.

What is the kernel of truth in this wise compassion?

What aspects can you take fault for?

What are the things that set you off?

Why were those things hurtful or even triggering?

Are there any threads that you can pull on to find greater revelations about consistencies in your own behavior?

What were you trying to accomplish?

How did this situation play out differently than you expected?

Did you accomplish what you wanted or needed?

How can you apply yourself differently in the future so that everyone can get what they need?

Similarly, when practicing wise compassion with someone that you care about, it's about easing into it.

Why is this person's behavior concerning to you?

What do you think they were trying to accomplish?

What concerning patterns can you see in their behavior?

Why do you think they reacted the way that they did?

How are they acting out of accordance from your values?

How are they acting out of accordance with their own values?

Did you accomplish what they wanted or needed?

How can you couch your concerns in compassion and bring up the issue to this person?

STAGNATING LEADERS

Power comes from authority

Privatizes information

Discourages team from developing ideas

Dictates solutions to problems

EFFECTIVE LEADERS

Power comes from collaboration

Shares information

Encourages suggestions and ideas

Collectivizes solutions to problems

Minimizes time & resources for problem solving	Allocates time and resources to prevent problems
Believes in strict roles & responsibilities	Roles and responsibilities are fluid and evolve
Deals reactively to problems	Resolves root causes of problems
Reviews staff performance once per year	Provides immediate and ongoing feedback and personalized coaching

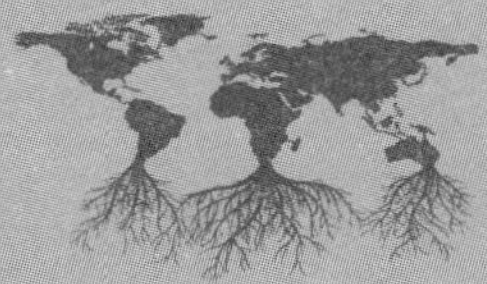

© Joe Biel, 2019, JoeBiel.net. This poster and other infographics like it are available from www.Microcosm.Pub

CONCLUSION

Accountability isn't a process that you do once and then you're done—being an accountable person is a lifelong habit. We hope that the tools in this book have given you a sense that this is possible for you. We know how hard this can be, and we also know how worthwhile it is.

You've done a lot of work in this book. Congratulate yourself. It's a lot to think about. If you are still feeling like you haven't connected all of the dots, don't beat yourself up. We'd say that doesn't signal failure, it signals the fact that you are recognizing that this is a complex and long-term process.

And because it can't be overstated, we want you to remember that accountability is a fundamentally personal process. It's not about what others say you should or need to do. It's aligning your actions to your values and recognizing your impact on the world. It's recognizing that your intentions do not always have the intended impact and that that is what is most notable to others. Sometimes this is as simple as getting to know yourself, admitting your mistake, and apologizing. Sometimes it's a years-long process to understand your motivations and behaviors that you see inside yourself and feel like you have no control over to change your outward expressions and patterns. For habits that took years to form, it can take years to change them.

Most people spend years of their life finding that it's easier to get their wants met than their needs and having trouble prioritizing their needs as a result. By accepting these things, working to repair them, and learning how to prevent patterns from forming or continuing in the future, we become who we want to see ourselves as.

Accountability is understanding why others see you the way that they do and what part of that is within your power to change. And taking accountability is ultimately going to be one of the most important actions that you can take in directing your life. Regardless of what attracted you to this book, please, do this work for yourself, not for other people or for specific relationships. If you're still breathing, it's not too late.

And if you think letting go of old thinking and patterns is difficult, wait until you see how difficult holding on was. Review, repeat, and challenge yourself every day.

Please send us your success stories.

Accountability Self Assessment

You've come so far. After all of these exercises, it's time to do the self-assessment again. When you're finished, go back and compare these answers to the ones you made at the beginning.

I am aware of my personal value system, and work to act in accordance with these values.

1 —————— 2 —————— 3 —————— 4 —————— 5

I know what motivates me, and use those focal points to prioritize my time and energy.

1 —————— 2 —————— 3 —————— 4 —————— 5

I follow through on expectations I set for myself, even if no one is watching me or checking in with me.

1 —————— 2 —————— 3 —————— 4 —————— 5

I honor my commitments to others, even if they are not watching me or checking in with me.

1 —————— 2 —————— 3 —————— 4 —————— 5

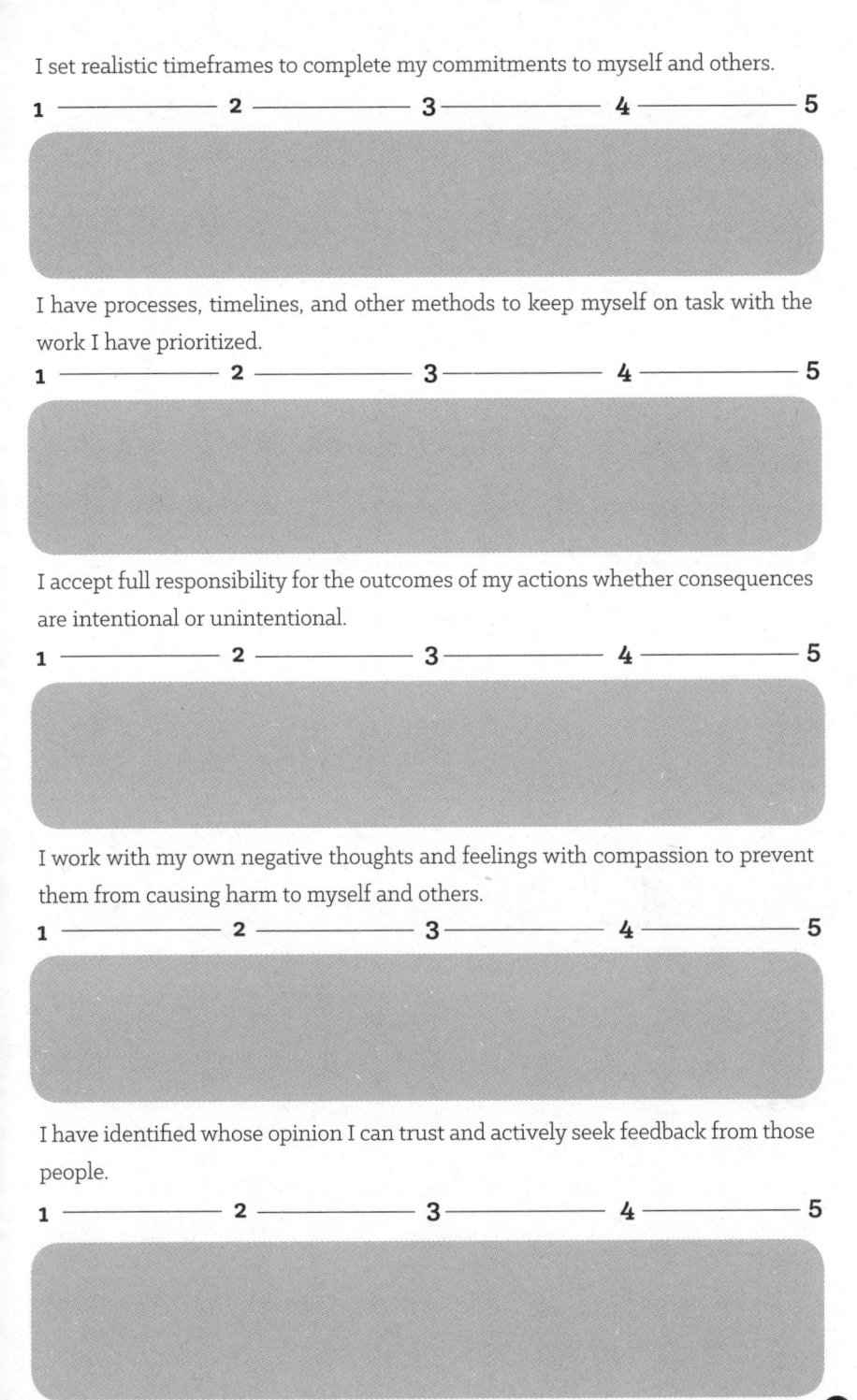

I set realistic timeframes to complete my commitments to myself and others.

1 —————— 2 —————— 3 —————— 4 —————— 5

I have processes, timelines, and other methods to keep myself on task with the work I have prioritized.

1 —————— 2 —————— 3 —————— 4 —————— 5

I accept full responsibility for the outcomes of my actions whether consequences are intentional or unintentional.

1 —————— 2 —————— 3 —————— 4 —————— 5

I work with my own negative thoughts and feelings with compassion to prevent them from causing harm to myself and others.

1 —————— 2 —————— 3 —————— 4 —————— 5

I have identified whose opinion I can trust and actively seek feedback from those people.

1 —————— 2 —————— 3 —————— 4 —————— 5

I accept constructive feedback even when it is uncomfortable and make appropriate adjustments to my behavior based on the feedback that has merit.

1 —————— 2 —————— 3 —————— 4 —————— 5

I evaluate my actions and the consequences of my actions regularly.

1 —————— 2 —————— 3 —————— 4 —————— 5

I focus on finding solutions rather than assigning blame.

1 —————— 2 —————— 3 —————— 4 —————— 5

I communicate with honesty.

1 —————— 2 —————— 3 —————— 4 —————— 5

I communicate with sincerity.

1 —————— 2 —————— 3 —————— 4 —————— 5

I endeavour to resolve conflicts directly with the concerned person or parties rather than complaining to third parties about the issue.

1 ———— 2 ———— 3 ———— 4 ———— 5

What's changed?

Do you think any of your assessments are more realistic now?

What are you most proud of?

Where did you have the most trouble?

What do you want to work on next?

More Dr Faith Harper from www.Microcosm.Pub

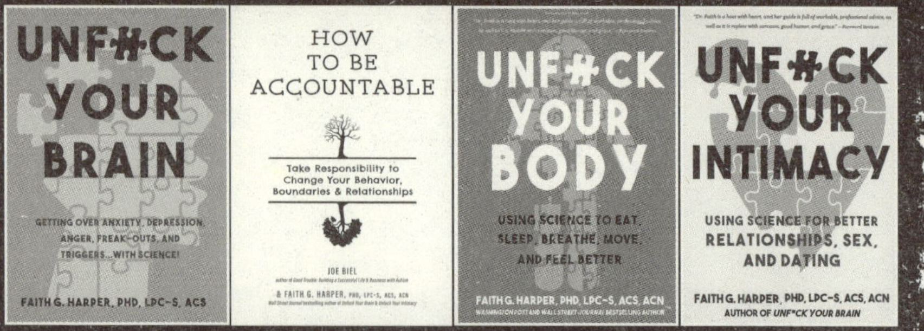

SUBSCRIBE!

For as little as $15/month, you can support a small, independent publisher and get every book that we publish—delivered to your doorstep!

www.Microcosm.Pub/BFF

More for becoming your best self at www.Microcosm.Pub

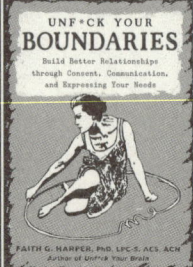